SCIENCE PRIMERS, *edited by*

Professors Huxley, Roscoe, *and* Balfour Stewart.

BOTANY.

Science Primers.

BOTANY.

BY

J. D. HOOKER, C.B., P.R.S.

WITH ILLUSTRATIONS.

London:

MACMILLAN AND CO.

1876.

151 . R . 147

PREFACE.

THE object of this Primer is to supply an elementary knowledge of the principal facts of plant-life, together with the means of training beginners in the way to observe plants methodically and accurately; and in the way to apply the knowledge thus obtained to the methodical study of Botany.

It is hoped that by its means the teacher may convey a sound elementary knowledge of the number, nature, relative positions and uses of the principal organs of plants, of the order and way in which they grow, and in which plants multiply, and of those resemblances which exist amongst them, by a comparison of which their true relationships are known and themselves classified.

In using this Primer the plants indicated are, whenever possible, to be put into each pupil's hand. Hence, to facilitate its use, I have placed at the end an Index of the plants referred to in it. These may be procured in the country, or from any intelligent nurseryman. Many of them should be grown in every school-garden, and arranged in it systematically, so that the teacher may have the same means of displaying to his pupils the principles of classification that the great founder of the natural classification of plants, Bernard de Jussieu, had after he had thus arranged the Garden of the Palace of Trianon after its establishment by Louis XV.

The teacher should further have a copious supply of dried flowers, and other parts of these plants so preserved as that the pupil can, after moistening them in warm water, separate their organs. Much may thus be learnt when fresh plants cannot be obtained, and a rehearsal of the summer's lessons upon such dried specimens is a most improving exercise. He should also have a supply of preserved fruits, seeds, sections of stems, and of mounted preparations of the tissues and minute parts of plants adapted for exhibition under the microscope.

Each pupil should have a pocket-lens magnifying three or four times, a sharp pen-knife, and a pair of forceps ; and he should be taught to preserve between sheets of paper the specimens he has examined, with a descriptive ticket attached ; and also be exercised in the habitual use of the schedules described at pp. 112, 113.

In using the Primer the pupil should be taught first, the contents of sections I. and II. ; after which he may either take the other sections in order, or go on to section VI., taking sections III. to V. afterwards. Sections XIX. and XXV. are too difficult for beginners.

After mastering its contents the pupil may proceed to the use of Professor Oliver's " Lessons in Elementary Botany," which goes over the same ground in more detail.

CONTENTS.

LIST OF ILLUSTRATIONS.

SCIENCE PRIMERS.

BOTANY.

I.—INTRODUCTORY.

THE study of Botany is best commenced with the careful observation of the different parts of living plants, their positions and arrangement in reference to one another, the order in which they make their appearance, and their uses to the plant itself. It is hence often called a science of observation, in contrast to Chemistry and other subjects of which the study must necessarily commence with experiment. But Botany is also an experimental science; only the experiments by which we investigate the growth of plants, their modes of living and multiplying, and their relations to the air and soil, require much to have been learnt first by observation alone. Such experiments require also for the most part a previous knowledge of Chemistry and Physics; those, however, described in this Primer will need no more knowledge of these subjects than is to be found in the Primers devoted to them.

Plants are living things; they form the Vegetable Kingdom as animals form the Animal Kingdom. Like animals, plants pass through the stages

of infancy, maturity, and death; they also feed, grow,
and multiply. Unlike the higher animals, during the
ordinary processes of growth (with the exception of
germination and flowering) they have no proper heat,
not being warmer than the air or water in which they
live.

Duration of Plant-life.—Some plants have
limited lives, flowering but once and dying soon after;
others have unlimited lives, throughout which they
flower periodically. Plants with limited lives are: 1.
Annuals, which live but for one year or season, as
wheat, peas, &c.; 2. Biennials which live for two
years, as the cabbage, turnip, foxglove, &c.; and 3.
plants which grow for many years without flowering
(for example many palms), flower but once, and
then die. Those with unlimited lives are Perennials,
and may be either trees and shrubs which, like the
oak and hawthorn, have stems and branches increasing
in size from year to year; or herbs like the primrose
and snowdrop, having underground root-like stems
which annually send up leaves or branches that die
off in the same year.

Distribution of Plants.—Plants are found on
nearly all parts of the surface of the globe, but no
two countries have all their plants alike. They are
found in the greatest luxuriance and variety in hot
and damp climates. They are not found in the
very coldest or very dryest regions, nor at very great
depths in lakes, or the ocean. As a rule, they
diminish in size, as well as in number of kinds in proceeding from the tropics to the frigid zones; as regards
size there are exceptions, as the gum-trees of South
Australia and the wellingtonia of California, which

are amongst the most gigantic of known plants; the seaweeds of cold seas are also far more bulky than those of tropical regions.

Besides the plants now growing upon the surface of the earth, the remains of many others that are no longer living anywhere, are found in rocks at various depths beneath it. Of these, those that lived most recently and are hence found in the more newly formed rocks, are like existing plants; those that lived longer ago are less like existing ones, and are sometimes very different looking indeed. In short, the longer ago the plants lived the less like they were to plants now living : but however different are the plants that lived longest ago, they all seem to have grown much in the same way, to have depended on similar conditions of light, heat, and moisture, and to have followed the same general course of life.

The Forms of Plants are infinitely varied. As trees, shrubs, herbs, grasses, ferns, &c., they are familiar to all; but only a small proportion of the Vegetable Kingdom consists of such plants. The bright green covering of banks, tree-trunks, damp walls, and cottage roofs, and the carpeting of forests and wooded valleys, chiefly consist of mosses and moss-like plants, of which several hundred kinds grow in Britain alone. The ocean's surface sometimes swarms with extremely minute plants, to such an extent as to give the water a distinct colour ; and its shores within and beyond the tide level are covered like gardens with sea-plants of many forms and colours. As green and purple slimes, plants also stain damp walls, and the rocks and stones in the bottom of fresh-water streams and along the seashore ; as leathery or

powdery crusts they cling to the hardest rocks and
stoniest soils of mountains and moorlands ; as moulds
they spoil articles of food, books, leather-work, woollen
and other fabrics; as dry-rot, and under many other
forms, they utterly destroy trees, wooden houses and
ships ; as smut, rust, bunt, potato- and vine-blight,
they prey upon the living tubers, stems, leaves, and
fruits of the most valuable crops, and some even
invade the organs of living animals.

Things Necessary to the Life of Plants are
air, heat above the freezing point, light, water, and
earthy (inorganic) matter in some shape.   The exceptions to this are few ; amongst them are the Red-
snow plant, a most minute vegetable, which tinges the
surface of melting snow with a rosy hue ; and fungi,
of which some grow or are cultivated in total darkness.   No plants, except these, continue to live in
health in the absence of light, as a few blind animals
can do (fishes and insects) which inhabit caves, as
well as many deep-sea animals, and those that live in
the interior of others.

The Division of Labour in Plants.—During
their life-time plants perform various kinds of work
which are essential, some to sustain them in life and
health, others to reproduce their kind.   These kinds
of work being very different from one another are not
accomplished by any portion of the plant indiscrimi-
nately but are carried on by particular parts specially
fitted for the purpose (called organs).

In the case of flowering plants, for example, the
principal **Organs** are, 1. The Root, by which the
plant is fixed to the ground, and absorbs nourishment
from it ; 2. The Stem, which supports the buds,

leaves, flowers, and fruit; 3. The Leaves, which are usually thin and so placed as to receive as much light as possible upon one surface ; 4. The assemblage of organs called the Flower; a part of this grows into the Fruit, which contains the Seeds.

The purposes which organs are specially fitted to serve are called their **Functions**. The most important of these in all plants are nourishment and reproduction. Plants have no organs of locomotion, or of the senses.

In Flowering Plants **Nourishment** is effected by means of the root and leaves. Unlike animals, such plants have no special stomach to receive the food, no heart or blood-vessels to distribute it, and no special organs to carry off what is not used as nutriment.

The **Food** of plants is liquid and gaseous, never solid. The root absorbs water, in which both gaseous and mineral matters are dissolved; and this fluid ascends and enters the leaves, which also take in carbonic acid gas from the air. By the action of light on the water and carbonic acid in the leaves a substance called **Starch** is formed, which is distributed throughout the plant, supplying in great measure the material for adding to its parts.

The excess of water taken up by the root is exhaled by the leaves, and this tends to keep them cool. From the starch produced in the leaves and nitrogenous compounds taken up by the roots and dissolved in the fluids which permeate the plant, **albuminoids** are formed, which are very essential in producing growth. These fluids further supply the materials from which are manufactured by the plant various substances, such as resin, sugar, oil, wax, and colouring matters.

The Reproduction of Plants takes place in two ways. First, and principally, by seeds; secondly by buds that separate and grow into independent plants. Seeds are produced by the interaction of special organs of two kinds, and are inclosed in a covering called the fruit. Buds that separate themselves and become new plants are formed on various parts of plants, as where the leaf is attached to the stem in the tiger-lily and the tubers or underground branches in the potato plant.

Many plants may be artificially increased by division; that is, by cutting off a twig with a bud on it, and sticking it into damp ground, when the twig will send forth roots. Or the twig may be inserted into a slit in the branch of a similar tree, with which it will unite, and the bud thus nourished will grow, and produce leaves, flowers, and fruits.

The Tissues of Plants.—The substance of plants is not, like a piece of stone, made up of particles in which no definite form or structure is visible, but is built up of minute bags called cells, and of tubes called vessels (which also consist at first of rows of cells), packed more or less closely together.

The Chemical Constituents of Plants.— Plants, like animals, contain a far greater weight of water than of anything else. Besides the elements of water (oxygen and hydrogen), the tissues contain carbon (which is the charcoal left after burning), and some also contain nitrogen. Plants obtain the water principally by their roots; the carbon by their leaves from the carbonic acid gas absorbed from the air, and the nitrogen in solution by the roots, from salts of ammonia (or nitrates). Most plants contain moreover small quantities of one or more mineral substances, also absorbed in solution by the roots.

The green colour which prevails amongst plants depends on the presence of a peculiar matter (**Chlorophyll**) within the cells, especially those near the surface of the plant. This matter is coloured green only by the action of light, consequently plants grown in quite dark places are never green, nor are those parts of them which are not exposed to the light (such as the roots). The lustrous hue and glossy appearance of most leaves is due to the fact of the coloured matter not being superficial, but inclosed in cells whose sides are usually as transparent as glass, and whose surface reflects the light.

The Primary Divisions of Plants.—Plants do not present a disorderly mass of living things, having no degrees of relationship one with another, like children's letters or numerals emptied out of a box; nor are they related to one another equally, differing in similar degrees, as one does from two, two from three, &c.; but they fall into groups variously related to one another, some like brothers, others like cousins, and so forth; whence arises the classification of the vegetable kingdom into sub-kingdoms, classes, orders, genera, and species.

There are two primary groups, or Sub-kingdoms of plants; the Flowering and the Flowerless, which differ very much indeed; the Flowering having, amongst other characters, usually very conspicuous structures commonly known as flowers, which produce seeds; and these seeds invariably contain an independent plantlet (embryo). The Flowerless plants (ferns, mosses, seaweeds, &c.) have no such flowers, nor such seeds : instead of seeds they have spores which contain no plantlet, but themselves grow into new individuals.

Plants purify the air that is being habitually rendered unfit to breathe by animals having already breathed it. They provide the animal kingdom with food, and often with shelter. They protect the surface of the earth from being too much scorched by the sun's rays by day, and too rapidly cooled by radiation at night. They prevent the too rapid evaporation of the rain-fall ; and they supply man with fuel, medicine, and many materials for arts and manufactures.

II.—GENERAL CHARACTERS OF FLOWERING PLANTS.

1. The Vegetable Kingdom as stated above presents two quite distinct Sub-kingdoms, which the most superficial observer rarely confounds : that of **flowering plants**, to which trees, shrubs, and herbs belong; and **flowerless plants**, such as ferns, mosses, seaweeds, lichens, and fungi.

The pupil is recommended to begin with the flowering plants, not only because the two sub-kingdoms are so different that they cannot be studied together advantageously by a beginner in Botany, but because the flowerless plants require for their study high magnifying powers of the microscope and great skill in using them.

2. Flowering plants present the following organs or

parts: **root, stem, leaves, flowers,** which latter
are succeeded by **fruit,** containing **seed.** Most
flowering plants have roots; all have stems, though
these may be reduced to a mere knob on the top of
the root: some few have no proper leaves, as the
dodder, and plants which, like it, feed on the juices
of others: many never have but one bud, which is a
flower-bud: but all must have a flower or flowers,
though these may be of a very simple nature.

3. The organs of flowering plants may be classed
according to their relation to one another under two
divisions: (*a*) an **axis,** of which the root is the
descending and the stem the ascending part; and
(*b*) **appendages of the axis,** which are the leaves,
and the parts of the flowers.

4. They may also be classed according to their
uses (**functions**) as follows: (*a*) for **support,** the
root and stem; (*b*) for **nourishment,** the root and
leaves; (*c*) for **reproduction,** seeds, buds that
separate from the plant, flowers, fruit.

This division is evidently a very rough one; for
while the root is often the sole organ of support,
fixing the plant to the ground and holding it upright,
other plants are supported wholly or in part by their
climbing or twining stems (convolvulus), by tendrils
(vine), by twisting leaf-stalks (clematis) and even
flower-stalks, by hooked prickles (brambles), by sticky
glands, and in the case of water-plants by floats
containing air.

The root and leaves are the chief organs of nutrition, but all green parts of the plant are so to
some extent.

The seeds are the principal means of reproducing

plants, but, as already pointed out, this process is also often effected by bulbs that separate themselves (tiger-lily) ; or by the budding of underground bulbs (onion) ; or by tubers covered with buds (potato).

III.—THE TISSUES OF PLANTS.

5. The substance or material of which a plant consists is called its tissue ; and there are several kinds of tissue. Their nature cannot be made out without a microscope ; but as a low power will show the most important of them, these should be learned at once.

6. The chief is **cellular tissue** (parenchyma),

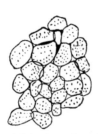
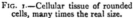
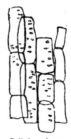

FIG. 1.—Cellular tissue of rounded cells, many times the real size.

FIG. 2.—Cellular tissue of rather long cells, many times the real size.

which forms the principal substance of most plants. It consists of minute oval sacs, called cells, crowded together and often becoming angular by pressure (Figs 1 and 2). Orange-pulp is an example of cells loosely packed together ; cork and elder pith of cells crowded together which have always been coherent by their sides. The walls of the sac consist usually of a very thin and transparent membrane, which may contain air only, when the cells are dead (as in pith); or a fluid, as in the cells of orange-pulp; or, besides fluid, granules of protoplasm (Par. 11), coloured by substances which are green in leaves, and of other tints in many flowers; or granules of starch. Sometimes the cell-wall is very thick and hard, as in the stone of the cherry and other stone-fruits, and the leathery surface of leaves such as those of the stone-

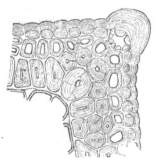

FIG. 3.—Thick-walled cells from a leaf of stone-pine as seen in a cross-cut, many times the real size.

pine (Fig. 3). Some plants are formed wholly of cellular tissue (mosses, fungi, seaweeds, lichens), and almost all plants have more cellular than any other tissue. Fluids can pass through the walls of the cells, and the nourishment which is sucked up by the roots in the fluid state, is distributed through the plant chiefly by passing from cell to cell. The cells which cover the surface of the plant are a good deal flattened, and form a layer called the **epidermis.**

7. **Wood-tissue,** of which in addition to v

wood is principally formed, consists of long cells, or rather tubes, tapering and closed at both ends, with thick walls, and which lie side by side and form wood.

8. **Bast-tissue** consist of very long flexible cells, or rather tubes, also closed at both ends. It occurs chiefly in the inner bark, and supplies the materials of many useful fabrics. Hemp and flax are bast-cells of the plants of those names; and the Bast, used by gardeners for tying, is the inner bark of the lime-tree.

9. **Vascular tissue** consists of long, unbranched tubes, with thin walls, which are often dotted or

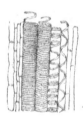

FIG. 4.—Spiral-vessels with cellular tissue on each side, many times the real size.

barred, and sometimes thickened internally by spiral threads, easily seen in the leaf of the hyacinth, if broken across. These are called spiral vessels (Fig. 4). All such tubes are formed from rows of super-posed cells, the partitions which separate them having been absorbed.

The tissues 7, 8, and 9 usually occur together in the form of bundles which traverse the cellular tissue, as the veins (or nerves) of the leaves, and are called **fibro-vascular bundles.**

IV.—THE GROWTH OF CELL-TISSUE, AND NATURE OF THE CELL.

10. To understand how plants grow, and how such products as sugar, starch, oils, resins, and medicinal substances are formed in them, it is necessary to examine further cellular tissue ; for it is by the addition of cell to cell that plants grow, and by chemical changes taking place within the cell, that the above-named and other substances are formed.

11. The cell consists of a wall (cell-wall) and its

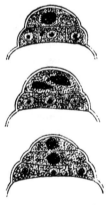

FIG. 5.—Growing point of stem of stonewort showing formation of new cells by division, many times the real size.

contents (cell-contents). The cell-wall is a thin (rarely thick) transparent bag of inert or *dead matter* called **cellulose** ; it contains when young a viscid granular substance *endowed with life* and sometimes exhibiting motion, called **protoplasm.** Cellulose is composed of oxygen, hydrogen, and carbon; protoplasm of these together with nitrogen.

12. When cells are very young they are smaller in size, the cell-wall is thinner, and they are completely filled with the protoplasm; a darker rounded portion of this is generally to be noticed in the centre and is called the **nucleus**. As the cells grow in size their cavity becomes larger than the mass of protoplasm which originally filled it. The cell-wall is always lined by a layer of protoplasm, but in the interior of the cell, cavities are formed in the protoplasm which are filled with a watery fluid called the cell-sap. Later on the protoplasm is reduced to a thin film, in which the nucleus is placed and which lines the cell-wall; strings of protoplasm pass from the nucleus across the cell-cavity. In old wood and cork cells the protoplasm has completely disappeared, and the cavity of the cell contains nothing but water or air.

13. New cells are formed by the protoplasm of some which are still quite young dividing into halves, between which a wall of cellulose is then formed. The original cell-cavity is thus divided into two. It is supposed that this breaking up of the protoplasm commences by the division of the nucleus seen in the protoplasm of most cells, and that the protoplasm collects round each half of the nucleus; but this is not certain.

14. The rate at which cells thus multiply is astonishing, and is most conspicuous in mushrooms, toadstools, &c., which are formed wholly of cellular tissue. The giant puff-ball grows in one night from the size of a marble to that of a child's head, by the growth and increase of cells, which individually are but a few

thousandths of an inch in diameter, and of which three millions are estimated to be formed in twenty-four hours.

15. Cells which have ceased to divide gradually grow into their permanent form, which in various cases is very different.

(a) Those of cork and pith do not alter very much in shape, and finally, losing their protoplasm and cell-contents which are absorbed into more active adjacent cells, simply contain air.

(b) Wood and bast-cells grow very much in length. The protoplasm continues to secrete cellulose which is added to the cell-wall and gradually makes it very thick (see Par. 6). These, too, lose eventually their living contents and contain only air or water. Other cells may have their walls thickened in the same way without becoming elongated. Vessels (Par. 9) are formed by the partitions between rows of superposed cells becoming absorbed.

(c) In many cases the protoplasm, instead of secreting thickening material which is added to the cell-wall, forms various substances out of the fluids which permeate through the cell-wall and mix with the cell-sap. These remain imbedded in the protoplasm, as in the case of starch grains, oily and fatty matters, or grains of albuminoids; or they are dissolved in the cell-sap, as in the case of sugar and the substances (alkaloids, &c.) which give so many plants useful or noxious properties.

(d) These substances often seem to fill the cell-cavity to the exclusion of everything else, but the remains of the protoplasm can generally still be traced, though in a very shrivelled state.

(*e*) In the green parts of plants the protoplasm undergoes a peculiar change, by which it is broken up into granules which contain the green colouring matter (chlorophyll). These granules are accordingly termed **chlorophyll granules**.

16. Chlorophyll granules, consist then of protoplasm coloured green by a pigment called chlorophyll. They abound in the superficial cells of plants, and their colour being seen through the thin cell-walls, give the green hue to leaves; similar granules tinged with other colours give in some cases the bright tints to flowers. Chlorophyll under the influence of sunlight brings about changes in the cells of the leaf that result in starch being formed and distributed all through the plant, as required. In so doing, it is supposed that the chlorophyll separates the carbon from carbonic acid taken from the air, gives back the oxygen to the air, and supplies the carbon (which at the same time combines with the components of water to form starch) to the plant. It is a curious fact that chlorophyll is not developed, and therefore that this process will not go on, except the plant be supplied with iron; and as all soils contain iron, the plant can always take this substance up by its roots. In the absence of sunlight also, the green colour of chlorophyll does not appear, hence celery is covered up to make it white, otherwise it is a very green plant.

17. **Starch.**—This compound of carbon, hydrogen and oxygen abounds within the cells of many parts of many plants, as the potato and all cereal grains, arrow-root, tapioca, sago, &c. It consists of white granules, differing in form in different plants (Fig. 6),

often marked with concentric rings, and is tinged bright blue with iodine. It is found in greatest quantity in the parts of plants intended to be deposits of food during winter, for the growth of the plant in the following spring. Seeds and roots, as they grow, use up the starch which the cells contain.

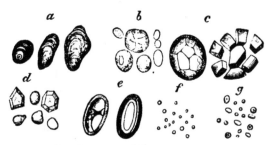

FIG. 6.—Starches. Granules of *a* Potato, *b* Wheat, *c* Oats, *d* Maize and Rice, *e* Bean and Pea, *f* Parsnip, *g* Beet; all very many times their real size.

18. **Oils** and **fats** are composed of the same elements as starch, from which they are probably manufactured by the plant, and as deposits of food serve the same purpose. Oils prevail in seeds and fruits, as linseed oil (from the seed of the flax-plant), cocoa-nut-, almond-, olive-, colza-, and castor-oils.

19. **Sugar,** formed also of the same elements, differs from all the preceding in being soluble in water, and existing only in solution. It abounds in the cells of sugar-cane, beet, parsnip, and all sweet fruits. It is formed out of the starch manufactured in the leaves.

20. **Albuminoids.**—These are compounds containing nitrogen in addition to carbon, hydrogen, and

oxygen. Gluten, the most common of them, occurs
in granules in the outer cells of wheat and other
grains. The viscid matter left in the mouth after
chewing wheat, especially hard wheats, is gluten.

21. **Alkaloids.**—These are very remarkable substances, which all contain nitrogen; many of them
are medicines, as quinine and morphia; others are
poisons, as strychnine and nicotine; still others have
stimulating properties, as theine and caffeine, to which
tea and coffee owe their refreshing qualities.

22. Other substances, of a **mineral** character,
enter into the composition of the cell and cell-
contents; as sulphur, which is a constituent of the
albuminoids; iron which, as already stated, is indis-
pensable for the production of chlorophyll; silica,
which is found deposited in the insoluble state
within the cell-walls; compounds of phosphoric acid,
which are associated in some way not understood
with the formation of albuminoids; and lastly, salts
of potash, which are concerned in a manner equally
unknown with the production of starch and sugar.
Other mineral constituents are found in the plant,
often in considerable quantity, such as salts of soda
in seashore plants. But this is due to their accidental presence in the soil; and marine plants
grown inland will usually flourish with very little
soda. Calcium, again, is very commonly present in
plants, being taken up from the roots as sulphate of
calcium. This, however, is decomposed by oxalic acid,
and oxalate of calcium, which is not readily soluble, is
formed, and this is deposited in the plant in the form
of crystals, while the sulphuric acid yields its sulphur
for the formation of albuminoids: these occur in

the cells of a walnut leaf (Fig. 7), and in rhubarb (Fig. 8), and beet (Fig. 9).

FIG. 7. FIG. 8. FIG. 9.

Crystals of oxalate of lime, as found in cells, many times the real size.

23. The great importance of the nitrogenous substance protoplasm, as the only living matter which the plant contains, cannot be too firmly insisted upon. It is of the same nature as the protoplasm of which some of the lowest animals (those nearest the plants) wholly consist, and which forms the living substance of the bodies of the higher animals, including man himself.

Like animals, plants cannot live without oxygen. The activity of the protoplasm in both cannot be kept up without it. The protoplasm of all living things wastes and would die altogether unless it were nourished. This process of nourishing involves **respiration,** *i.e.* getting rid of superfluous carbon, which combines with oxygen taken in from the air, and is given off as carbonic acid (Par. 158).

V.—THE FOOD OF PLANTS.

ABSORPTION, TRANSPIRATION, ASSIMILATION.

24. The food of plants is partly gaseous and partly liquid; and is derived from the earth or water in which they grow, and from the air. The liquid food is taken into the plants chiefly by their roots, the gaseous chiefly by their leaves.

25. The **gaseous food** of plants consists of carbonic acid gas, supplied chiefly by the atmosphere. The **liquid food** is water, in which various saline substances are dissolved, the principal components of these being nitrogen, phosphorus, sulphur, potash, and iron. The above-named matters are found in most soils in which plants grow, but cannot be taken up by the roots except they be dissolved in water.

26. **Absorption.**—The taking in of liquid food by the roots is called absorption, and the liquid absorbed becomes part of the sap in the plant. The sap ascends through the stem and branches, and so reaches the cells of the leaves, or the cells near the surface of plants that have no leaves. In mounting up it passes both from cell to cell through their walls and along some of the tubes of the vascular tissue.

The taking in of carbonic acid gas from the air is another process of absorption. It is performed by the leaves, in the cells of which a chemical process goes on under sunlight, by which the carbon is broken up, the carbon being retained by the plant, and the oxygen given back to the air. The carbon being at the same time combined with the oxygen and hydrogen of water as already explained (Par. 15, *c*), the substance known as starch is formed.

27. **Transpiration.**—The sap, cn reaching those surfaces of plants that are exposed to the light, parts with a great deal of its water as vapour, either through minute pores in the leaves, or through the walls of the superficial cells, as in the case of plants that have no leaves. These pores are called **stomates** (Par. 72); they exist in very great numbers, chiefly on the underside of the leaves; an apple-leaf presents upwards of 100,000 of them. This process of evaporation, called transpiration, keeps plants cool in the hottest weather, and is so rapid that a sunflower plant has been found to give off a quart of fluid in twenty-four hours, and an oak or beech-tree must give off many gallons in the same space of time.

28. **Assimilation.**—The process by which the carbonic acid absorbed by the leaves and the water absorbed by the roots are combined together in the leaves under the influence of sunlight to form starch, free oxygen being at the same time given off, is called assimilation. The starch so formed appears to be dissolved in the cell-sap during darkness, and to be distributed from cell to cell all over the plant. It is used up wherever growth is taking place, furnishing the material for the formation of the cellulose of the new cell-walls, or it is stored up again in the solid form as a reserve of material for future use, as in seeds. Besides conversion into cellulose, starch is capable of being transformed under the influence of protoplasm into oily and fatty matters, and also into sugar.

The soluble starch in its downward passage through the tissues of the stem, meets with various saline matters containing nitrogen, such as nitrates or salts of ammonia. From these in some way or other not yet understood, but under the influence of protoplasm, the nitrogen is abstracted, and from this, together with the constituents of starch, albuminoids are manufactured.

These albuminoids are the necessary food of protoplasm. It is important to remember that their formation depends upon the manufacture of starch in the green parts of plants, and this depends upon exposure to sun-light. We see, therefore, why without light plants starve; their protoplasm ceases to be nourished.

29. The effect of plants requiring mineral substances for their nourishment is, that one kind of crop cannot be grown continuously on the same piece of ground, if it is periodically cut and carried away. This has led to the use of manures containing the substances taken away in the crop, for rendering the exhausted soil fit for another crop of the same kind. In a state of nature, on the contrary, the plants of each piece of ground die where they grow, and by decay give back to the soil what they took from it.

30. The above-mentioned plant-foods are all inorganic substances; and until quite recently plants (except fungi and parasites) have been supposed to be incapable of deriving nourishment from organic substances except these be completely decayed. It is now, however, ascertained that some plants can derive nourishment from raw meat, insects, and other animal and even vegetable matter, such plants being provided with organs for the purpose of digesting such matters. The leaves of the nepenthes, side-saddle flower, venus's fly-trap, and sundew, are instances. In all

these cases where the meat is laid on the digesting
surface, a fluid is poured out from its cells which
acts as a solvent on the animal substance, enabling
the plant to absorb it and use it for its nourishment.

31. Except in cases of accident, plants in a state
of nature either die a natural death, that is, one that
comes after the functions of all its organs have been
fulfilled, or are eaten by animals.   Those that die
a natural death undergo chemical changes which
constitute decay, and in so doing return to the air
and earth the materials of which they were con-
structed.   Those that are eaten by other animals
undergo quite a different set of chemical changes in
the animal's body, and which may be said to result
in the several constituents of the plant supplying
nitrogenous substances to the animal's muscle, carbon
to its fat, mineral matter to its bones.   These, or
some of these, are necessary to the life and health
of every animal, and are what it cannot obtain from
simple inorganic substances except these have been
first taken up by plants and united together into more
complicated compounds.

VI.—THE GROWING SEED.

GERMINATION.

32. It is well to commence the actual study of
plants by that of the growth of the seed, as it is very
easily observed, and a right understanding of the early
history of the plant as studied in its seedling state is
a great help to the learner of its later history.

33. Take seeds of pea, mustard, and wheat, and
place them on dry earth.   So long as earth and seeds

remain dry the seeds will not grow. Moisten them
and put them where the temperature does not rise
above freezing; still they will not grow. Place them
in a vessel from which all air is excluded; still they
will not grow. Lastly, place them where the temperature is considerably above freezing, and where
air has access to them, and keep them moist, and
they will grow, whether in light or shade. This
growth of a seed is called its **germination.**

34. From these experiments we learn that to produce
germination in a live seed, water, air, and a heat con-

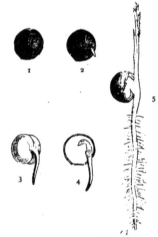

FIG. 10.—1 Pea, 2 Radicle pushing through Integument, 3 Embryo with
Radicle elongated, 4 the same with one Cotyledon removed, 5 the same
further advanced ; all twice the real size.

siderably above the freezing point are all required.
And what is thus proved of the seed applies to plants
throughout their lives—namely, that to grow they

must have warmth, air, and moisture. Further on it will be shown that to grow to maturity light is also wanted; but at present we are concerned only with the germinating seed.

35. From experiment now proceed to observation. All seeds consist of two principal parts—a dead part outside and a living part within it. The living part is the **plantlet**, or **embryo**, and is in fact an im-

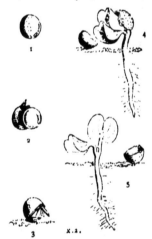

Fig. 11.—Germination of Mustard, 1 Seed, 2 Embryo removed from Integument, 3 Radicle pushing through Integument, 4 Cotyledons and Radicle after throwing off Integument, 5 Young Plant; all twice the real size.

mature plant, having a separate existence from that of its parent: the dead parts are its coverings (**integuments**), together with sometimes a nourishing matter (**albumen**) provided for the plantlet, and like it contained within the integuments. The pea and mustard have no albumen; the wheat has.

36. The **plantlet** consists of several parts, which serve different purposes. In the pea (Fig. 10) it consists of two thick masses (**cotyledons**) placed face to face and united at one point of their margins. A small cylindrical body lies between the cotyledons where these unite, and is attached to them about its middle. It is conical at one end, and blunter

FIG. 12 —Wheat germinating : 1 Seed cut vertically, showing—*a* the integument. *b* the albumen. *c* the embryo ; 2 the same further advanced ; 3 back view of grain, with *d* plumule, and *e* sheathed rootlets ; 4 the same further advanced ; all twice the real size.

at the other. When the seed grows, the conical end (the **radicle**), which lies below the point of junction with the cotyledons, elongates downwards and gives origin to the root of the plant. The blunter end (the **plumule**), which lies above that point, elongates upwards and becomes the stem of the plant; the scales are undeveloped leaves. To ascertain which is the radicle and which the plumule of the plantlet, the seed must sometimes be examined soon after it has germinated, when they are easily distinguished, whether by their form or by the directions they take.

37. This elongation of plumule and radicle is the first growth made by both the pea and the mustard but after this they follow quite different modes of development.

In the case of the pea the cotyledons do not grow at all, but supply nourishment to the growing radicle and plumule, which absorb it through the points of union; after which, their nourishing matter being exhausted, the cotyledons shrivel and dry up, or rot. The plantlet thus feeds on the same substance as is eaten at table, and in so doing it empties the cells of the cotyledons of the starch, oils, albuminoids (Sect. 17 to 20) which they contained. Here, then, the cotyledons nourish the plumule and radicle from the very first.

In the case of the mustard, on the other hand, whilst the radicle plunges into the soil, the cotyledons are carried up above ground, where they spread out to the light, become green, and assimilate for the plantlet, as leaves do for full-grown plants.

38. In the wheat (Fig. 12), the plantlet lies on one side of the seed, between its integument and the albumen, which is white and floury. It has not two opposite thick cotyledons, but one, which forms a sheath around the other leaves of the plumule. When germination begins, the plumule and radicle absorb nourishment from the albumen by contact, and not through a connecting structure such as that which unites the

plumule and radicle of the pea to its cotyledons. The plantlet here feeds on the flour of which we make bread, just as the pea plantlet fed on the part of the pea which we eat.

The radicle of the wheat does not elongate upon germination, as that of the pea and mustard did, but rootlets grow out from it with sheaths at their base.

39. These great differences between the cotyledons, the growth of the root, and the mode of germination of the pea (or mustard) and of the wheat, are most important, being characteristic of the two great divisions (classes) of flowering plants, called **Dicotyledons** (plants with two cotyledons or seed-leaves) and **Monocotyledons** (plants with one cotyledon or seed-leaf), which divisions are further to be recognized by other characters hereafter to be described.

VII.—THE ROOT.

40. The root is formed by one or more prolongations of the radicle of the embryo (Sect. 36). Its uses to the plant are, to fix it to the ground, to absorb nourishment from the latter, and sometimes to store up and retain nourishment during winter for the food of the plant during its growth in the following spring.

41. Roots are known from stems by their growing downwards from the plantlet (Sect. 36), and usually afterwards avoiding the light; by their not, or very rarely, bearing buds; and by their structure and mode of growth.

42. When only a single prolongation of the radicle is formed this is called a **tap-root.** This bears at its

side numerous slender branches or **root-fibres.**
Sometimes the **tap-root** is very insignificant and not
easily distinguished from its fibre-like branches ; the
whole root is then distinguished as fibrous. **Root-
fibres** are usually so slender that it is not easy to
see their nature ; but this can be done in the hyacinth
root, the tip of which, if cut down the middle shows

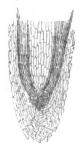

FIG. 13.—Vertical section of tip of Root-fibre of Hyacinth, many times the
real size.

under a microscope that a sheath of soft flattened cells
envelops the tip, within which is a mass of denser
cells which form the growing point.

43. Root fibres do not push themselves into the
soil as one thrusts a stick into it ; but they push their
way through interstices in the soil as they elongate
at the point. As the root fibre elongates, the front
part of the sheath decays, and the back part, which
is constantly renewed by the growing point, takes
its place ; thus advancing and displacing water in
the case of the hyacinth, and earth in other cases.

In shrubs and trees the root-fibres as well as the
tap-root thickens as it grows, becomes woody, and
displaces the earth laterally as well as in front ; and

with such force does growth go on that it is common
to see stones of walls displaced by roots.   In tropical
countries the destruction of buildings is universally
caused by the power of growing roots ; and neither
conquering nations, nor earthquakes, nor fires, nor
tempests, nor rain, nor all put together, have de-
stroyed so many works of man as have the roots
of plants, which have all insidiously begun their work
as slender fibres.

44. Nourishment is taken in by the **root-hairs,**
but not by the growing-point.   Root-hairs are delicate
long cells, that stand out from the surface of the
elongated radicle and of the root-fibres, and may be
seen on the first formed root of the pea and mustard
plants in great quantities.

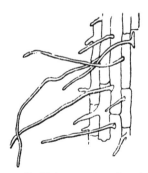

FIG. 14.—Root-hairs, many times the real size.

45. Roots may be roughly classed under two heads
—those that simply nourish the plant as it grows, and
those that lay up a store of nourishment to assist the
growth of the plant during the second year.

To the first class belong (*a*) the very simple annual

roots that consist wholly of simple fibres (hyacinth);
(*b*) annual roots of much branched fibres (grasses,
groundsel, shepherd's purse); (*c*) branched roots whose
fibres become woody in the second year (trees, shrubs,
and herbs with woody roots).

To the second class belong (*a*) such roots as
are fleshy and globose or spindle-shaped (turnip,
carrot, radish, beet). These produce leaves the first
year, and in the second, leaves, flowers, and fruit,
after which the whole plant dies. They are nourished
by slender fibres from their sides and tip. (*b*) Roots
with many fleshy branches, called tubercles (ficaria,
dahlia). (*c*) Roots with only two fleshy tubercles like
the orchis, which deserves a separate description.

46. The root of an orchis consists of two distinct
fleshy tubercles, one large, the other small. Both

FIG. 15.—Tubercles and Root-fibres of Orchis.

grow at the bottom of the stem, below the stout root-
fibres which spread horizontally from just above them.
When an orchis is in flower, the flower-stem proceeds
from the top of the large tubercle, which bears the
smaller tubercle attached close to its neck. Later in

the year, when the orchis is seed-bearing, the large
tubercle will be found withered, and the little tubercle
to have grown large and plump, and have a bud at
its top. Still later, the whole plant dies, except the
smaller tubercle with its bud, which latter will grow
up as the orchis stem of the next year. An English
orchis plant is thus a travelling store of food, which
makes a little journey annually; but in Australia certain
orchises make a much longer annual journey, for the
new root-tubercle, instead of being attached to the
base of the stem close to the old root-tubercle, is
attached to the latter by a root-fibre sometimes six
inches long; and such orchises make comparatively
rapid marches under the ground.

47. **Adventitious Roots.**—Root-fibres may in
some cases be thrown out from the stems of plants.

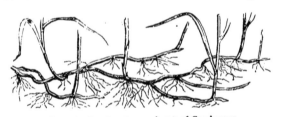

FIG. 16 —Creeping stems and roots of Couch-grass.

Such rootlets are called adventitious, and are found
on mature plants of both Monocotyledons (stem of
couch-grass near the ground), and of Dicotyledons
(wall-roots of ivy), and they form the supports of the
branches of the banyan-tree of India.

VIII.—THE STEM.

48. The stem is formed by the elongation of the plumule of the embryo (Par. 36); its uses are to support the leaves, buds, and flowers, and to form a channel of communication by which the water absorbed by the roots is conveyed to them, and the starch formed in the leaves is distributed over the plant.

49. The stem usually seeks the light, but not always; for many stems grow underground, elongating, and even branching horizontally; such stems (cowslip, potato) are often mistaken for roots, from which they differ in their mode of growth, and in bearing leaves, buds, and flowers.

50. A fully developed stem may be simple (most palms) or branched. It consists of **nodes** and **internodes** : the nodes are the points from which leaves arise; the internodes are the intervening portions of the stem or branch. The nodes are swollen in many plants (pinks, grasses); in grasses the internodes are usually hollow while the nodes are solid.

51. The chief modifications of the stem besides the common erect one are—

The **twining** stem (hop, honeysuckle, convolvulus), of which some turn to the right, some to the left; but very rarely does one kind of plant turn either way indifferently. This twining habit is the effect of an inherent disposition in the tips of all elongating stems to bend successively towards all the points of the compass; a movement which is very obscure in plants with straight stems, but very marked in those that climb. The tip of such a stem, as it elongates, describes a wider and wider sweeping circle, till the stem strikes a support, when the portion above the point of contact with the support continuing to revolve as it lengthens, naturally twines round and ascends it. Such stems, if they find no support, become weak as they lengthen, and fall on the ground.

52. The principal underground forms of stem are—

(*a*) The **bulb,** a very short, usually underground stem, with excessively crowded, overlapping leaves. These leaves are wrapped round one another in the onion, but simply overlap in the tiger-lily.

(*b*) The **rhizome** or root-stock, a woody underground stem, which sends root-fibres from its lower side, and buds and leaves from its upper side (iris). The **corm** is a very short fleshy rhizome (colchicum).

(*c*) **Bulbils** are small bulbs or corms formed at the side of old ones, and are hence analogous to branches, under which they will be further noticed.

53. The tissues of the stem of flowering plants are arranged on two plans, one characteristic of Dicotyledons, the other of Monocotyledons (Par. 39). These plans must be understood by the pupil, and can be so by a little patience and practice with specimens ; they are best illustrated by three such examples as the flax, lime, and butcher's broom, or asparagus.

54. The flax plant (a Dicotyledon) has an erect herbaceous stem of many internodes (Par. 50), with leaves all the way up, and flowers at the ends of the branches.

A magnified cross-cut of the stem shows that it consists of a cylinder of cellular tissue (Par. 6), traversed vertically by a ring of wedge-shaped fibro-vascular bundles (Par. 9), which are separated from one another by the cellular tissue. The central cellular tissue is the future pith, that at the circumference is the future outer bark, and that between the fibro-vascular bundles is the future silver-grain of wood. The fibro-vascular bundles are in part future inner bark and in part future wood, and consist of wood-tissue (Par. 7) mixed with vascular tissue (Par. 9) towards the centre, and of bast-tissue (Par. 8) towards the circumference. Of these components of the vascular bundle the bast-tissue forms the inner bark; the wood and vascular tissues form the wood of the plant. Such is the origin of outer bark, inner bark, wood, pith, and silver-grain.

A cross-cut of a one year's old twig of lime shows the same arrangement of tissues as the flax; but whereas the flax stem dies the same year as that in which it is formed, the lime twig lives through the winter, and is added to during the following summer, increasing thus in thickness.

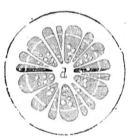

FIG. 17.—Transverse section of vascular bundle from stem of a Dicotyledon.

FIG. 18.—Transverse section of stem of a Dicotyledon.

55. This increase of thickness is caused by new tissue being added between the bast and wood formed in the previous year. This new tissue consists at first of soft, tender, cellular tissue, produced by the growth

of the **cambium layer** (which lies between the bast
and the wood) in spring, in the position indicated;
and which after the leaves expand, and are acted upon
by light and heat, gives rise to an additional layer of
new bast-tissue inside the old bark, and new wood-
tissue with vascular tissue amongst it outside the old
wood.

56. Omitting details (such as the formation of layers
of cellular tissue outside the bast-tissue), this is the
plan upon which the stem and branches of all plants
with two cotyledons are formed. It has been called
Exogenous growth, because the bulk of the stem is
increased by additions to the outside of the wood.
Exogenous plants are hence synonymous with Dicotyledons (Pars. 39, 53).

57. The branch or stem of a dicotyledonous tree
or shrub (as the lime) if more than one year old, hence
consists, proceeding from the centre, of (*a*) pith;
(*b*) layers of wood (with a little vascular tissue), of
which the oldest layers are next the pith; (*c*) layers
of bast-tissue, of which the oldest are next the circumference; (*d*) layers of cellular tissue, of which the
oldest are next the circumference; (*e*) rays of cellular
tissue stretching from the pith to the circumference.

58. The pith of the centre never grows after the
first year; but the cellular tissue of the outside of the
bark often grows by annual additions between it and
the bast layers, and of that the barks of the cork,
plane and birch trees afford conspicuous examples.

59. The stem or branch of the butcher's broom,
or asparagus (Monocotyledons), has a totally different
structure. A cross-cut shows that the whole consists
of a cylinder of cellular tissue, traversed by isolated

bundles of fibro-vascular tissue (Par. 9), not arranged in a ring, or in concentric rings, but scattered without order through the cellular tissue, and much crowded at the circumference of the stem. Each of these isolated bundles consists outwardly of bast-cells and

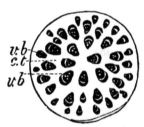

FIG. 19.—Transverse section of stem of a Monocotyledon.

inwardly of wood-cells, exactly as in the first year's stem of flax or lime (Par. 54). These bundles do not, however, increase by the addition of bast-cells and wood-cells.

60. Commencing at the bases of the leaves, all the fibro-vascular bundles of a Monocotyledon may be traced downwards, first arching inwards towards the centre of the stem, then gradually outwards to its circumference, where they are closely crowded. There is hence no true bark, though sometimes the cellular tissue surrounding the vascular bundles forms a separable outer layer, as in the dragon-tree (*Dracæna*), in which also new bundles are formed which are disposed in concentric rings as in Dicotyledons (Par. 56). In all cases, however, the individual bundles are not added to as in Dicotyledons, and they are hence called definite bundles.

61. The arrangement of vascular bundles above de-scribed is characteristic of Monocotyledons (Par. 39).

IX.--BUDS AND BRANCHES.

62. Buds are formed in autumn, either at the ends of stems and branches, or at the angle where the leaf or leaf-stalk meets the stem, and remain dormant till spring. They have wood, pith and bark continuous with those of the stem, with which their union is hence complete. They are usually protected from cold and wet by scales that are often covered with gum or with hairs.

FIG. 20.—Leaf-buds and vertical section of ditto.

Some plants increase only by terminal buds (willow, elm); others by both terminal and axillary buds (horse-chestnut, ash, and most trees).

63. Buds become leafy branches by the develop-

ment of their internodes (Par. 50), and may produce
leaves only, or flowers, or both ; or they may in some
rare cases fall away from the plant (tiger-lily), and
form new plants, sending roots downwards and stems
upwards.

If the terminal bud produce only an inflorescence
(Par. 75) its onward growth is stopped, and lateral
buds form below it and are developed into permanent
branches.   This takes place in the horse-chestnut
and lilac, and gives an angular character to their
branching.   In many half-woody plants, the branches
grow on indefinitely till killed by the winter's cold,
when buds form low down on the stem which develop
similar branches in the following spring.

64. Buds may, instead of simply elongating into
branches, grow in width and form short fleshy tubers,
of which the potato is an example.   A careful examination of a potato plant shows that it consists of an
underground branched ascending stem, which bears
root-fibres, and shortened fleshy tuberous branches
(the potatoes), covered with eyes, which are buds in
the axils of undeveloped leaves.   The bulbils at the
side of the bulb of a hyacinth or crocus are buds.

65. The **tendrils** of the Virginia creeper are modified branches whose divisions expand at their tips
into glue-tipped suckers, that fix the branches to the
wall.   The tendrils of the grape-vine are also branches
with spirally-twisted thread-like divisions, which on
finding a support twine round it, following the same
course as twining stems (Par. 51).   The **spines** of
most plants are stiff shortened branches (hawthorn,
sloe).   (Prickles are quite different things, and will be
explained in Par. 138 (*e*).)

66. The branching of trees forms a most admirable winter study, and one full of interest. It is sufficient to allude to the zigzag branchlets of the oak, with rounded terminal buds ; the graceful, straight twigs of the beech, with lancet-shaped buds ; the bold stout branchlets of the horse-chestnut, with ovoid buds; and the exquisite subdivided sprays of the elm, like lace-work against the sky. All these characteristic features are due to the form, direction, and setting on of terminal twigs and buds, and are objects of equal interest to the botanist and the artist. Leafless branches of the common English trees suspended against a white wall are capital studies for pupils, and reveal characters that escape the observation of teachers whose attention has not been called to them.

X.—LEAVES.

67. Leaves are expansions of the cellular-tissue of the stem traversed by fibro-vascular bundles (Sect. 9). Their use is to afford a large surface for exposing to the action of sun-light and heat the food absorbed by the plant and thus cause assimilation (Par. 28) ; they also provide for evaporation (Par. 27) ; and they absorb the carbonic acid of the air (Pars. 26, 28).

68. The external characters of leaves are very various indeed, and are characteristic of whole groups as well as of individual kinds of plants. The following principal facts regarding the leaves of some common plants should be observed by the pupil :—

(*a*) As to duration. Whether they are deciduous, falling annually; or persistent, continuing a year or longer.

(*b*) As to position. Whether in opposite pairs (dead-nettle, maple, horse-chestnut); or alternate (lime, ivy, grasses); or whorled (woodruffe, bed-straw); or tufted (larch, cedar, pine).

(*c*) As to insertion. Whether by a stalk (**petiole**) (lime, &c.), or not (**sessile**), or by a **sheath** (grasses); and whether the petiole is inserted at the bottom of the blade, as in most plants, or in the centre, as in the penny-wort.

(*d*) As to division. Whether **simple** (lime, ivy, oak), or **compound**—that is, formed of separate pieces (**leaflets**), (ash, horse-chestnut, rose, pea, bean).

(*e*) Whether their margin is **entire** (privet); or **serrate**, with teeth pointing upwards (lime); or **toothed**, with teeth pointing outwards (holly); or **lobed** (ivy, oak); or **cut** (hawthorn); or **pinnatified**, cut on each side to the middle (dandelion); or **multifid**, cut repeatedly into little segments (parsley, milfoil).

(*f*) Whether **stipulate**—that is, having appendages at the base of the petiole (*c*) called **stipules**, which may be persistent (rose, pea, heartsease), or deciduous, that is, soon falling away (apple, oak, beech); or if they are **ex-stipulate**, having no stipules (privet, box).

(*g*) If compound (*d*). Whether the leaflets (*d*) are **digitate**, spread out like the fingers (horse-chestnut); or **pinnate**, having the leaflets in opposite or alternate pairs, in which case there is sometimes a terminal leaflet (ash), and sometimes none (pea).

(*h*) Other characters, relating to form, texture, surface, colour, smell, are too numerous and detailed be employed as exercises for the observation of the beginner, who should be able to apply all those terms mentioned above to the trees and shrubs of his county.

69. The way in which leaves are folded together, or doubled up, or rolled up in bud, is called their **vernation**, and is an excellent subject for the pupil's observation. Thus, in grasses and in the cherry they are simply rolled round one another; in the apple they overlap in opposite pairs; in the flag they are sharply folded upon one another; in ferns they are rolled inwards from the top like a crozier; in the pear and apple the margins of each leaf are rolled inwards, and in the rosemary and the willow the margins are rolled backwards; in the vine, beech, and gooseberry, each leaf is plaited.

70. The chief substance of all leaves is cellular tissue (Par. 7), continuous with that of the stem. The cellular tissue is traversed by fibro-vascular bundles (Par. 9), also continuous with those of the stem. The leaf tissues are thus, like those of the bud (Par. 62), in complete union with those of the stem.

71. A cross section of a leaf shows, beginning at the upper surface (*a*), a delicate skin (**epidermis**) (Par. 6) of flattened transparent cells; (*b*) a layer of close packed cells full of green chlorophyll granules (Par. 16); (*c*) several layers of loosely packed cells with air-spaces between them; (*d*) an epidermis similar to that of the upper surface.

The vascular bundles consist of bast-tissue towards the under surface of the leaf, and wood-tissue, with vascular tissue, usually consisting of spiral vessels, towards the upper surface.

72. The epidermis is studded with breathing pores, **stomates** (Fig. 21), which usually consist of two sausage-shaped superficial cells inclosing an oval orifice. The stomates of most plants open more widely in the light than in the dark, and this must have the effect of promoting evaporation (Par. 27).

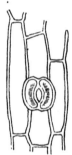

Fig. 21 —Fragment of Epidermis with a Stomate.

The glass-like sheen of the surface of leaves is due to the texture and transparency of the epidermis under which the cells full of green chlorophyll granules are seen (Par. 16).

73 The **venation,** or arrangement of the vascular bundles in the leaf, is for the most part very different in Dicotyledons and Monocotyledons. In the former, one or more vascular bundles enters the petiole (or the leaf itself if sessile), and usually either runs to the end of the blade as a mid-rib, or sends a branch into each division of the leaf; while from each side of this mid-rib branches are given off that branch again, and by uniting form a network. In most Monocotyledons either many vascular bundles enter the leaf and run

lengthwise through the blade, meeting at its tip, or
one such bundle splits up at the base of the leaf into
many that run as above ; in most Monocotyledons
these main bundles are connected by straight transverse bundles. To these rules there are exceptions,
but they are sufficiently constant to make it always
worth the while to examine the venation of a leaf
together with the characters given in Pars. 39, 53,
and 60, when referring a plant to one of these two
classes.

74. The death and separation of the leaf previous
to its fall from the parent plant are not accidental,
but due to the following causes :—

First, and chiefly, because there is developed at
the base of the leaf, or its stalk (if it has one), a
transverse layer of cells destined to die after the leaf
has performed its functions and before any other
part of the leaf does so. The leaf consequently falls
off, leaving a clean scar. Secondly, because the leaf
rapidly acquires in spring its full size, whilst the branch
on which it grows goes on thickening ; consequently,
the tissues at the point of union tend to become
disunited. Thirdly, because the fluids taken in by
the root go to the leaves ; these fluids contain earthy
matter, most of which is deposited in the leaf
tissues, choking them, preventing them from per-
forming their functions, and hastening their death.
This is proved by burning spring leaves, which yield
little ash, while autumn leaves yield more even than
wood does. It is however remarkable that the substances contained in falling leaves are those which
have ceased to be of value to the plant. The starch
and protoplasmic substances, together with the most

on the peduncles are called **bracts,** those at the base
of or on the pedicels **bracteoles**; the bracts at the
base of or around a head or umbel or flower, are often
crowded together, and form an **involucre**, which may
consist of one whorl of leaves (carrot), or of many
overlapping bracts (daisy, acorn-cup).

XII.—THE FLOWER.

80. The use of the flower is to bring about the
multiplication of the plant by seed.

81. The flower consists of one or more series of
organs crowded round the tip of a peduncle or pedicel
(Par. 76), and called **floral whorls.**   These differ
greatly in form, colour, and size; but all bear the same
relation to the stem as leaves do, and are modifications of the leaf-type.   All foliar organs are developed
on one plan, but take different shapes and perform
different functions according to the requirements of
the plant.

82. Before describing the individual floral organs,
it will greatly facilitate the student's progress to fami-
liarize him with their number, form, and relative
positions, in flowers which differ very widely from
one another.   Beginning from without, the floral
whorls are :—

(*a*) **Calyx,** a protective organ; it forms the first or
outer whorl, is usually green, and its pieces, called
sepals, may be separate (free), or combined into
a cup or tube, wholly or in part only.

(*b*) **Corolla,** an attractive organ; it forms the
second whorl; it is white or coloured (very rarely
green) in order to attract insects to the flower : honey

is often exuded at particular points within it. Its
pieces, called **petals**, may be free or combined into
a cup or tube, or into the form of a bell, a funnel, &c.

(*c*) **Stamens**, usually slender organs, form the
third whorl, they consist of a stalk (**filament**), sur-
mounted by a 2-lobed body, the **anther**, containing
a fine yellow-powder, the **pollen**, necessary to per-
fecting seeds. The filaments may be absent or combined into a tube, or into bundles, or be altogether
free, as may the anthers.

(*d*) The **Pistil**, or central organ, forms the innermost or fourth whorl, and presents many more modifications than any of the preceding. In its simplest
form (pea) it represents a leaf folded down the middle
with its edges united so as to form a hollow vessel
(**ovary**); the tip tapers into a stout or slender body
(**style**), which terminates in one or more rough or
moist, often swollen nobs or surfaces or points
(**stigmas**). The style may be absent, when the
stigma is sessile on the ovary.

The pistillar leaf is called a **carpel**, and its cavity
contains, attached to its inner surface, one or more
minute bodies, destined, after fertilization (by the
action of the pollen on the stigma), to become
seeds. The pea-pod is one such carpel with several
ovules. The buttercup has many such carpels, each
with one ovule, style, and stigma. When there are
several carpels they may be free (buttercup), or combined by their edges into a one-celled ovary (violet),
or by their sides into an ovary with as many cells
as carpels (lily). In these cases of united carpels the
styles may be free or combined; and when combined, the stigmas may still be free. The number of

carpels of which a pistil is formed, when these are combined, may often be assumed from the number of cells of the ovary, or of styles or of stigmas.

(*e*) The floral **receptacle** is the tip of the flower-stalk which bears the floral organs. The **disk** is a thickening of the receptacle between the pistil and corolla or calyx; it is often swollen (rue, lime), and secretes honey; or it is represented by scales or small prominences. The stamens may be inserted around it, or on it, or between it and the ovary.

83. If a flower contains all four floral whorls (Par. 81), it is called **complete**; if fewer, **incomplete**. The calyx and corolla together form the **perianth**; also when the calyx is undistinguishable from the corolla, or when either of these is absent, the outer floral whorl takes the name of perianth.

Of the floral whorls, the calyx is seldom absent, the corolla less seldom. The stamens and pistil cannot both be absent, but one may be: in this case the missing whorl will be found in correspondingly incomplete flowers borne on the same or some other individual plant. Very few flowers have fewer than two sepals or two petals, but many have either no stamens or no pistil; and a flower may consist of a single stamen or a single pistil.

An **irregular** flower is one in which one or more of the parts of the calyx or corolla is larger than another (pea, snap-dragon). A **regular** flower is one in which this is not the case, but the members of each whorl are equal and similar.

A **symmetrical** flower is a regular one whose sepals, petals, and stamens are equal in number or multiples of one another.

B.P.   E

84. The principal modifications of the flower depend on (*a*) the absence of one or more of the above whorls, and the form of those that exist ; (*b*) on the members of each being free or combined ; (*c*) on the members of one whorl being adherent to those of the one next outside or inside of it ; (*d*) on the position of each whorl upon the receptacle. Of these modifications, the most obvious is that the ovary is sometimes placed above the calyx (buttercup, Fig. 22), and sometimes apparently below it (snowdrop, daffodil, Fig. 37). In the latter case, the appearance is caused either by the ovary being sunk in the top of the flower-stalk, and becoming one body with it, or by the lower part of the calyx adhering to the walls of the ovary; in either case the corolla, disk, and stamens are carried up above the level of the ovary, and are as it were inserted upon it. The rose (Fig. 31) and apple (Fig. 32) are obvious examples of the ovary being sunk in the top of the flower-stalk.

85. The flowers enumerated below are now to be examined, and the pupil taught to name the organs of each and their uses ; this done, the organs should be described according to their modifications. In doing so, attention should first of all be given to the following points :—

(*a*) Whether the flower is complete, (Par. 83); if not, which whorls are absent.

(*b*) The number of members of each whorl, and whether they are opposite or alternate with the members of the whorl outside it.

(*c*) Whether the members of each whorl are free, or combined together, and whether they adhere to those ˚ the whorl outside or inside of them.

(*d*) Whether the flower is regular or irregular (Par. 83).

(*e*) Whether the flowers are **bisexual,** having both stamens and pistil (buttercup), or **unisexual,** having one only of these; and if the latter, whether the flowers that bear the stamens are **monœcious,** that is, on the same individual with those that bear the pistil (oak, nut), or **dicœcious,** that is, on another individual (willow, common nettle).

(*f*) Whether the calyx is above the level of the ovary or below it.

A.—Complete flowers with inferior perianth (the calyx and corolla being below the ovary).

Buttercup (Fig. 22).—Flower regular. Calyx of 5 free sepals. Corolla of 5 free petals alternate with the

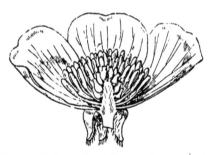

FIG. 22.—Vertical section of Buttercup flower, enlarged.

sepals. Stamens many, seated on the receptacle. Pistil of many free carpels.

Bramble (Fig. 23).—Flower regular. Calyx of 5 sepals combined at the base. Corolla of 5 free petals. Stamens many, seated on the calyx. Pistil of many free carpels. (Note the different insertion of petals and stamens of buttercup and bramble.)

FIG. 23.—Vertical section of Bramble flower, enlarged.

Wallflower (Fig. 24, 25).—Flower rather irregular. Calyx of 4 free sepals, two inserted lower down than

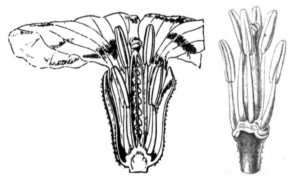

FIG. 24.—Vertical section of Wall-flower, enlarged.

FIG. 25.—Stamens of Wall-flower, enlarged.

the others.   Corolla of 4 free petals.   Stamens 6, two
shorter than the others, and placed opposite the lower
sepals.   Pistil of 2 carpels combined into a 2-celled
ovary with a very short style and notched stigma.

Pink.—Flower regular, with many bracts.   Calyx
of 5 sepals combined into a 5-cleft tube.   Corolla
of 5 free petals alternate with the sepals.   Stamens
10, five alternate with and five opposite to the petals.
Pistil of 2 combined carpels forming a 1-celled ovary
with 2 styles.

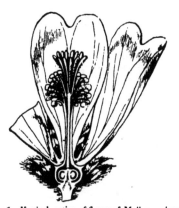

FIG. 26.—Vertical section of flower of Mallow, enlarged.

Mallow (Fig. 26).—Flower regular, with 3 bracts.
Calyx of 5 free sepals.   Petals 5, alternate with the
sepals, combined below.   Stamens very many, filaments combined into a tube which adheres at the
base to the petals.   Pistil of many carpels combined,
with many combined styles with free stigmas.

Pea (Fig. 27).—Flower irregular.   Calyx of 5 combined sepals.   Corolla of 5 very unequal petals of
which the two innermost are combined.   Stamens 10,
9 united and 1 free.   Pistil of 1 carpel, with 1 style
and stigma.

Fig. 27.—Section of flower of Pea, enlarged.

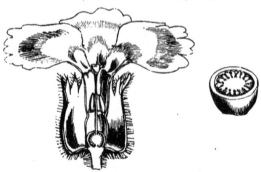

Fig 28.—Vertical section of flower of China   Fig. 29.—Transverse sec-
        Primrose, enlarged.   tion of ovary, enlarged.

Primrose (Fig. 28, 29).—Flower regular. Calyx of 5 combined sepals. Corolla of 5 petals combined into a tube below. Stamens 5, opposite the petals, their filaments combined with these. Pistil with a 1-celled ovary having 1 style and stigma.

Deadnettle (Fig. 30).—Flower irregular. Sepals 5, combined into a cup. Corolla of 5 petals com-

FIG. 30.—Vertical section of Dead-nettle flower, enlarged.

bined into a tube with two lips ; lobes alternate with the sepals. Stamens 4, 2 longer than the others. Pistil of 2 carpels forming a 4-celled ovary with 1 style and cleft stigma.

B.—Complete flowers with superior perianth.

Rose (Fig. 31).—Flower regular. Calyx of 5 sepals. Corolla of 5 free petals, alternate with the sepals. Stamens many, seated on the calyx. Pistil of many separate carpels sunk in the hollowed top of the pedicel.

Fig. 31.—Vertical section of Rose, enlarged.

Apple (Fig. 32).—Flower regular. Calyx of 5 sepals. Corolla of 5 free petals, alternate with the sepals. Stamens many, seated on the calyx. Pistil of 5 combined carpels, each with a style.

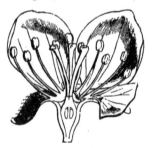

Fig. 32.—Vertical section of Apple flower, enlarged.

Gooseberry.—Flower regular. Calyx of 5 sepals. Corolla of 5 free petals. Stamens 5, alternate with the petals, seated on the calyx. Pistil of 2 carpels combined, forming a 1-celled ovary with 2 styles.

Campanula.—Flower regular. Calyx of 5 sepals. Corolla of 5 combined petals alternate with the sepals. Stamens 5, alternate with the petals, seated on the top of the ovary. Pistil of 3 or 5 carpels combined into a 3- or 5-celled ovary, with 1 style and 3 or 5 stigmas.

Elder.—Flower regular. Calyx of 5 sepals. Corolla of 5 combined petals alternate with the sepals. Stamens 5, seated on the corolla and alternate with the petals. Pistil of 2 combined carpels with 2 cells and 1 style and stigma.

Honeysuckle.—Flower irregular. Calyx with 5 minute teeth. Corolla of 5 petals combined in a tube. Stamens 5 seated on the corolla, alternate with the petals. Pistil of 3 combined carpels with 3 cells and 1 style and stigma.

Daisy (Fig. 33, 34).—Flower of 2 forms in a compact head surrounded by green bracts. *Outer*

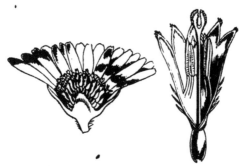

FIG. 33.—Vertical section of head of Daisy, enlarged.   FIG. 34.—Inner flower from head of Daisy, enlarged.

flowers unisexual, irregular, white. Corolla white, of 5 petals combined into a narrow long ray. Stamens o.

Pistil with 1 cell 1 style and 2 stigmas. *Inner flowers* bisexual, regular, of 4 or 5 petals combined into a yellow tubular 4-5 cleft corolla. Stamens 4 to 5, seated on the corolla, anthers combined. Pistil as in the outer flowers.

C.—Incomplete flowers, having an inferior perianth.

Dock.—Flower regular. Perianth of 6 nearly free pieces. Stamens 6, seated at the base of the perianth, alternate with the perianth pieces. Pistil of 3 combined carpels with 1 cell and 3 styles.

Daphne (Fig. 35).—Flower regular. Perianth of 4 combined pieces. Stamens 8, seated on the perianth, 4 upper opposite, 4 lower alternate with the perianth pieces. Pistil of one 1-celled carpel with 1 style and stigma.

FIG. 35.—Vertical section of Daphne flower, enlarged.

Tulip (Fig. 36).—Flower regular. Perianth of 6 free pieces. Stamens 6, opposite the pieces of the perianth. Pistil of 3 carpels combined into a 3-celled ovary with 1 style and a 3-lobed stigma.

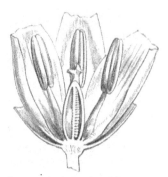

F<small>IG.</small> 36.—Vertical section of Tulip flower.

D.—Incomplete flowers having a superior perianth.

Daffodil (Fig. 37).—Flower regular.   Perianth of
6 pieces with a raised crown.   Stamens 6, seated on

F<small>IG.</small> 37. –Vertical section of Daffodil flower.

the base of the perianth opposite its pieces. Pistil of 3 combined carpels with 3 cells and 1 style and stigma.

Orchis (Fig. 43).—Flower irregular. Perianth irregular of 6 pieces. Stamen 1, combined with the style. Pistil of 3 carpels combined into a 1-celled ovary.

E.—Flowers without an obvious perianth.

Willow (Fig. 38, 39).—Flowers in catkins (78). Catkins of two kinds on different plants, both formed of overlapping scales; those of one kind of catkin overlying each one or more stamens; those of the other catkin overlying each a single pistil. Pistil of 2 carpels combined into a 1-celled ovary with 2 styles.

Fig. 38.—Male flower of Willow, enlarged.   Fig. 39.—Female flower of Willow, enlarged.

Wheat (Fig. 40).—Flowers in spikelets consisting of 2 minute scales (the perianth), 3 stamens and 1 pistil, the whole inclosed in two sets of green bracts. Pistil with 1 cell and 2 styles.

Fig. 40.—Spikelet of Wheat, enlarged.

86. It has been already stated that the above organs of a flower are all formed on the plan of leaves, but modified for different purposes. The best evidence of this is afforded by, (*a*) the calycanthus, which shows the transition from leaves to bracts, from bracts to sepals, and from sepals to petals; by (*b*), the white water lily, which shows the transition from sepals to petals, and from petals to stamens; (*c*), the garden rose, and most double flowers, which show the transition from petals to stamens; (*d*), the double tulip, which shows the transition from stamens to pistil; (*e*), the

double cherry, in which the carpels appear as green leaves.

87. The number of sepals, petals, and stamens is in Dicotyledonous plants, most frequently 4 to 5 each, or a multiple of that number ; whereas 3 or a multiple of that number prevails in Monocotyledons ; which is the fourth means of distinguishing plants of this class (see Pars. 39, 53, 60, 73).

XIII.—THE CALYX.

SEPALS.

88. The calyx is formed of a whorl of free or combined organs called **sepals.** It is usually green and leaf-like in texture, and it often persists in the fruit. Its use is to protect the parts of the flower within it.

89. Although the outermost of the floral whorls, the calyx is sometimes placed at a higher level than the ovary. This is because either the ovary is sunk in the swollen top of the peduncle (rose, Fig. 31); or because the surface of the sepals adheres more or less to the sides of the ovary, their free parts spreading out above it. Hence the employment of the terms calyx superior and calyx inferior, which are equivalent respectively to ovary inferior and ovary superior (Par. 84 *d*).

90. The sepals of the calyx may be free from one another, when the calyx is polysepalous (butter-cup, Fig. 22) ; or combined, when it is monosepalous (primrose, Fig. 28).

91. The most curious form of calyx that commonly occurs is that of the dandelion, groundsel, thistle,

and other plants with their flowers in heads (Par. 78*c*).
Here the ovary is inferior, and the superior calyx is
represented by a tuft of fine hairs, called a **pappus.**

Fig. 41.—Dandelion fruit with
pappus, enlarged.　　　　Fig. 42.—Thistle fruit with pappus.

The valerian has a similar calyx. In these plants the
feathery calyx assists in the dispersion of the fruit.
The calyx may take some of the irregular shapes to
be described under the Corolla.

XIV.—THE COROLLA.

PETALS.

92. The corolla is formed of a whorl of free or
combined organs called **petals.** It is usually coloured
and thin, and much larger than the calyx; it is often
scented, and soon fades, rarely persisting in the fruit
(which it does in the campanula). Its use is to attract
insects and birds to flowers for the purpose of fertilizing

them (Sect. XX), and it also often protects the parts of the flower within it. The many colours of flowers, their various shapes and scents, and their honey, are so many baits, for insects especially.

93. The corolla is inserted on the receptacle (Par. 82 *e*) in the butter-cup; on the calyx in the apple (Fig. 32) and rose (Fig. 31); in flowers with a superior calyx (campanula), apparently on the top of the ovary, but really on the calyx or peduncle, where these become free from the ovary.

94. The petals of the corolla may be free from one another, when the corolla is polypetalous (buttercup, Fig. 22); or combined, when it is monopetalous (primrose, Fig. 29).

FIG. 43.—Spotted orchis-flower, enlarged.

95. The so-called irregularity or regularity of flowers (Par. 83) depends mainly upon the form of the corolla, and has reference to the visits of insects, &c. for the

purpose of fertilization. Of these irregular forms the most common monopetalous one is the mask-like or personate (snap-dragon, dead-nettle, Fig. 30); and the most common polypetalous one is the butterfly-shaped or papilionaceous (clover, pea, Fig. 27). The latter is so characteristic of a very large family of plants (pea family) that names have been given to its five petals; the upper being called the standard, the two side ones wings, and two within them, which are often combined by their lower margins, form the keel. If the visits of bees to irregular flowers are watched, it will be seen, in very many cases, that the form of the corolla is singularly adapted to facilitate the insect entering it in order to obtain honey for itself, when it also carries away pollen from the stamens (Par. 123).

96. The commonest regular monopetalous corollas are the bell-shaped (campanula), funnel-shaped (convolvulus), salver-shaped (primrose), and wheel-shaped (pimpernel). In these, as in the regular polypetalous corollas (apple, Fig. 32, buttercup, Fig. 22), there is little or no relation between the form of the flowers and those of the insects that visit them. In some instances however of regular monopetalous flowers, there is a special adaptation of the organs of the flower to those of the insect, as where the corolla has a long tube and the insect a long proboscis; the bee and primrose is an example (Par. 122).

97. Petals are formed of a thin plate of cellular tissue traversed by vascular bundles (Par. 9). Their colouring follows certain rules. The corollas of few or no plants present all the primary colours, and white alone is found in all families of plants with coloured corollas

White and various shades of yellow and red are found in roses, tulips, and rhododendrons, but never blue. Blue, yellow and white are found in gentians, but very rarely red. Anemones are amongst the few plants in the different kinds of which red, yellow, blue, and white are found. Night-flowering plants have usually large, white, very strong-scented corollas, on purpose to attract moths. Certain lurid red or purple flowers both look and smell like putrid meat, and hence attract flies, which lay their eggs on them and fly away with the pollen.

98. Honey when secreted on the corolla is usually at its very base (honeysuckle, crown-imperial), and to reach it the insect has to disturb or brush against the stamens, and hence carry away pollen. In the grass of Parnassus, the honey is secreted in the tips of the branches of an elegant comb-like scale opposite each petal. The glands that secrete the honey are called **nectaries.**

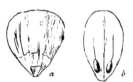

FIG. 44.—Honey glands of, *a*, buttercup; *b*, barberry; both enlarged.

XV.—THE DISK.

99. Usually at the base of the stamens and around that of the ovary, there is a thickened ring of cellular tissue, or a whorl of swellings, scales, or glands. It very often secretes honey when the corolla does not,

and is a part of the floral receptacle (Par. 82*e*).   In
the buttercup (Fig. 22) there is no disk; in the bramble
(Fig. 23) it forms a thickened shining lining of the
base of the calyx ; in the orange (Fig. 45*a*) and mignonette (Fig. 45*b*) it forms a distinct cushion ; in the

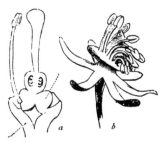

FIG. 45.—Disks of, *a*, orange ; *b*, mignonette : both enlarged.

wallflower it appears as two moist honeyed glands
at the base of the short stamens ; and in the carrot
and similar flowers it crowns the ovary.

XVI.—ÆSTIVATION.

100. As the folding together of the leaves in bud is
called vernation (Par. 69), so that of the floral organs
is called æstivation.   In this folding that of the sepals
never interferes with that of the petals, and these
often follow quite different plans.   These plans are
constant throughout the flowers of any one kind of
plant, and the same plan prevails through many allied
plants ; in other words, æstivation is a guide to the
detection of relationships amongst plants.

101. There are four principal plans of æstivation.
1. **Imbricate,** when one or more pieces are outside

the others, which others may all overlap by one margin, or one of them may be inside all the others (petals of apple). 2. **Twisted**, when each overlaps by one margin the contiguous margin of that next to it (corolla of periwinkle, convolvulus). 3. **Valvate**, when they meet by their edges without overlapping (calyx of mallow). 4. **Open**, when they grow quite apart, neither overlapping nor touching (petals of mignonette).

Fig. 46.—Æstivations: *a*, imbricate; *b*, twisted; *c*, valvate, with the edges turned outward.

102. The stamens usually grow straight from the first, but are sometimes curved or rolled inwards (myrtle and nettle), or backwards (kalmia).

XVII.—THE STAMEN.

ANTHER, POLLEN, FILAMENT.

103. The stamen consists essentially of the **anther,** a 2-lobed, 2-celled organ filled with granules (the **pollen**); its lobes are placed right and left to the axis of the flower. The anther may or may not have a stalk (**filament**), which contains a vascular bundle (Par. 9) that terminates between the anther-lobes. The use of the stamen is to form, contain, and discharge the pollen.

104. Stamens are variously inserted, but always within the calyx and corolla and outside the pistil, if these be present. They vary in number, and may be in one or more series; when equal in number to the petals or divisions of the perianth, they usually alternate with these in Dicotyledons, but are opposite to them in Monocotyledons; when twice as many they are alternate and opposite. They are inserted on the receptacle in the buttercup (Fig. 22), on the calyx in the bramble (Fig. 23), on the disk in the lime, on the corolla in the primrose (Fig. 29), and are combined with the pistil in the orchis (Fig. 43). The filaments are free in most plants; more or less combined in the mallow (Fig. 26); combined by bundles in St. John's wort; nine are united together and one is free

Fig. 47.—Stamens of pea, nine combined and one free; enlarged.

in the pea (Fig. 47). The anthers are usually free, but combined in the thistle and daisy, the filaments being free.

105. The anther in its early state is a cellular 2-lobed body, with longitudinal rows of special cells in the centre of each lobe. The contents of each of these special cells (called mother-cells) divide into four, which form as many pollen grains. These pollen grains acquire first one and then a second cellulose- (Par. 11) coat, and finally escape from the mother-cell and lie loose in the cavity of the anther.

106. When fully formed the anther-cells open to allow the pollen to escape, in most plants by longitudinal slits on the face (towards the pistil) ; but in some by lateral slits (buttercup), or dorsal ones (iris). In the heath order the anthers open by terminal pores (Fig. 48 *b*), which in the bilberry (Fig. 48 *a*) are at the end of long tubes. In the barberry (Fig. 48 *c*) they open

Bilberry.   Heath.   Barberry.   Mistletoe.

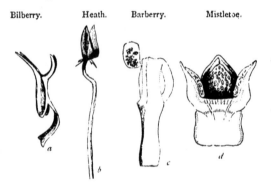

FIG. 48.—Stamens of. *a*, bilberry ; *b*, heath ; *c*, barberry ; *d*, mistletoe : all much enlarged.

by oblong lids that fall away ; and in the mistletoe (Fig. 48 *d*) by many holes, each of which is a pocket full of pollen.

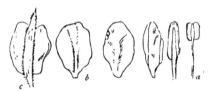

FIG 49.—Transition from stamen *a*, to petal *b*, and to sepal *c*, in double rose.

107. The relation of the stamen to the leaf is not so clear as are those of the sepals, petals, and carpels; nevertheless the transition from petal to stamen is obvious in the white waterlily, and in many double flowers, as the rose (Fig. 49).

Fɪɢ. 50.—*a*, pollen grains of orange ; *b*, pollen grains of buttercup upon the stigma with their tubes descending to the ovule ; both very much enlarged.

108. The **pollen** grains are usually globose, or ellipsoid, or rounded with obtuse angles ; they are generally free, but sometimes escape from the mother-cell connected in fours (rhododendron). In orchis they escape as club-shaped masses (Fig. 57). The surface of the granules is smooth, sculptured, or prickly, and this and their size and shape are wonderfully constant in each kind of plant, and through many allied plants.

A pollen-grain consists of two cellulose coats and fluid protoplasmic contents. When placed on the stigma (Par. 112), one or more tubes formed of the inner cellulose coat are pushed through slits or holes in the outer, and descend through the stigma an' style to the cavity of the ovary, finally conveying protoplasmic fluid from the pollen to the ovule.

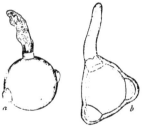

FIG. 51.—Pollen grains of, *a*, evening primrose ; and *b*, cherry ; both emitting pollen tubes—very greatly enlarged.

XVIII.—THE PISTIL.

OVARY, STYLE, STIGMA.

109. The pistil is by far the most complicated organ of the flower, and consists of one or more carpellary leaves (Par. 82 *d*). If it is composed of many such leaves, these may be so combined as to form a one- or many-celled ovary. Its use is to produce within its cavity **ovules,** destined to become seeds, and to provide means for conducting the contents of the pollen to the ovules.

110. The **ovules** are generally produced on the edges of the carpellary leaf; which presents a spongy thickening called the **placenta,** to which the ovules are attached by a short or long cord or stalk called the **funicle.**

The position of the placenta depends on the composition of the pistil; if the latter is formed

of one carpel (pea, Fig. 27) the placenta will be on
the walls of the cavity of the ovary (parietal); so also
if two or more carpels are united by their edges only
(Fig. 53), the ovules will still be parietal; but if two
or more carpels are closed by the infolding of the
edges of the carpellary leaves as far as the axis of the
pistil, and are combined by their sides into one,
the ovules will be on the axis of the pistil or on
placentas projecting from it (Figs. 36, 37, 52).

FIG. 52.—Axile ovules.

FIG. 53.—Parietal ovules.

111. The **style** consists of a column of cellular
tissue continuous with the midrib and margins of the
carpellary leaf or leaves, enclosing a core of looser
cellular tissue amongst which the pollen tubes (Par.
108) descend to the ovary.

112. The **stigma** occupies the top, or the sides of
the top of the style; or of the ovary if there is no
style, and is not covered with epidermis (Par. 6),
which would obstruct the descent of the pollen tubes.
It is frequently formed either of short loose cells
which exude a viscid fluid that holds the pollen grains,
and hastens the protrusion of their tubes; or of long
cells, forming tufts of hair, amongst which the pollen-
grains become entangled.

XIX.—THE OVULE.

113. The **ovule** is a minute body enclosed in the ovary, and destined, after being fertilized by the pollen, to become a seed, and to contain an embryo or plantlet. There may be one, few, or many ovules in an ovary; and if there are two or more, all, or a few, or one only, of these may be fertilized and become a seed.

114. In its earliest stage the ovule consists of a **nucleus**, which is a most minute swelling of cellular tissue formed on the placenta (Par. 110). Next a ring of cellular tissue grows up around the base of the nucleus and all but envelops it, leaving a canal or hole (**micropyle**). Often a second ring forms at the base of the first, and is similarly developed into an outer covering. A vascular bundle (Par. 9) runs from the edge of the carpellary leaf through the placenta into

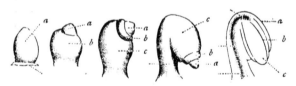

FIG. 54.—Growth of ovule of celandine : *a*, nucleus ; *b*, first formed covering ; *c*, second covering—very greatly enlarged.

the ovule, reaching the base of the nucleus, and is concerned in its nutrition and in that of the seed.

115. The ovule may be straight, or it may grow obliquely, or it may as it were turn round on itself by the greater growth of one side, so as to become com-

pletely inverted, when the micropyle, instead of being
distant from the placenta, is brought into proximity to
it, and the base of the nucleus is at the top of the
ovule. In this last case the vascular bundles from the
placenta run up the side of the ovule to base of
the nucleus.

116. In the axis of the nucleus, a cavity lined with
a delicate membrane (the **embryo sac**) containing
protoplasm, appears. Within this sac again near its
top a dark spot is seen (**germinal vesicle**), which,
after the application of the tip of the pollen tube to

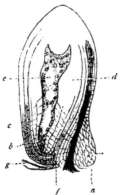

FIG. 55.—Longitudinal section of ovule of heartsease : *a*, placenta ; *b*, outer
coat ; *c*, inner coat ; *d*, nucleus ; *e*, embryo sac, with the germinal vesicle
at its small end ; *f*, micropyle ; *g*, end of pollen-tube—very much enlarged.

the nucleus, acquires a cellulose coat, and becomes a
cell. This cell, by division (Par. 13), gives origin
to a filament, from the end of which the embryo is
developed.

XX.—FERTILIZATION.

117. Though stamens and pistil frequently occur in the same flower, it does not follow that the pistil of such a flower is fertilized by its own stamens. On the contrary, it has been proved by many careful observations and experiments that nature has provided that pistils should be fertilized by pollen from other flowers, or from the flowers of other plants. Hence some plants bear stamens and pistils on separate flowers of the same individual (oak, hazel); others have stamens and pistils on different individuals (willow); in others again, when stamens and pistil occur in the same flower, they do not become mature at the same time; and in still others, when stamens and pistil do occur in the same flower and are mature at the same time, they are so placed in reference to one another or to the corolla &c., that the pollen cannot reach the pistil.

118. It has also been proved, that, as a rule, a pistil fertilized by the pollen of another flower, or that of another individual of its own kind, produces more and larger seeds which grow into stronger plants, than if it had been fertilized by the pollen of its own flower.

119. These and many other observations tend to prove that the elaborate structures, colours, scents, honeyed secretions, and other attractions of the corolla, stamens and pistil, and their adjustments to one another and to the forms and habits of insects, are all intended to prevent flowers from being fertilized by their own pollen, and to facilitate their being fertilized

by pollen brought from other flowers.   This operation
is called cross-fertilization.

120. In respect of fertilization flowering plants may
be roughly classed under two heads, according as
the pollen is carried to the pistil by the wind or by
insects.

Wind-fertilized plants have, as a rule, stamens and
pistil in different flowers or individuals.   Their flowers
are not bright-coloured, are scentless, and have no
sugary secretions, and their stigmas are covered with
hairs that retain the pollen ; in some the anthers hang
out of the flower (plantain, poplar, willow, oak); their
pollen is abundant, dry, and powdery (birch, alder,
pine).

121. Insect-fertilized plants, on the other hand, present innumerable contrivances to ensure the fertilization of the pistil by pollen from another flower or
plant, of which the following examples must suffice.

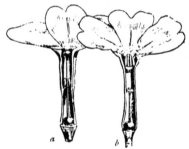

F<small>IG.</small> 56.—Vertical section of corolla of, *a*, long-styled, and *b*, short-styled
primrose.

122. The primrose has two sorts of flowers, which
never occur on the same plant ; one has the stamens

far down the corolla tube, and the stigma high up at
its mouth, the other has stamens high up the tube and
the stigma far down; both have honey at the very
bottom of the corolla tube.   When a bee visits a
short-styled flower, it thrusts its proboscis to the
bottom and, withdrawing it, brings away some pollen
at its base.   If it then visits another short-styled
flower it cannot fertilize it, and only takes more pollen
away; but if it visits a long-styled flower it must deposit pollen on its stigma, that being at the mouth of
the corolla.   If, on the other hand, the bee first visits
a long-styled form of primrose the operation is reversed,
it will then carry away pollen upon the tip of its
proboscis and deposit this on the stigma of the next
short-styled flower it visits.

123. In the common orchis the anther is placed ·
above the stigma, which is a hollow viscid cavity in
front of the flower, at the base of the lip, and the lip
is produced into a long tube full of honey.   A bee
seeking honey thrusts its head against the anther, and
in so doing detaches one or both of the two sticky
glands to which two club-shaped masses of pollen are
attached; these it carries away on its forehead, in
an erect position.   So long as the pollen masses
are erect on the bee's head these do not reach the
stigma of any other flower that it visits; gradually,
however, as the sticky gland contracts, the pollen
masses incline forward and assume a horizontal
position, in which they must touch the stigma of
the next flower the bee visits, when the greater
stickiness of the stigma detaches some or all the pollen from the bee's head and fertilizes the flower.
Further, in some cases it takes so long for the pollen

to assume the horizontal position, that by the time this has taken place the bee has visited all the flowers of the plant from which it took the pollen, and has gone to another plant.

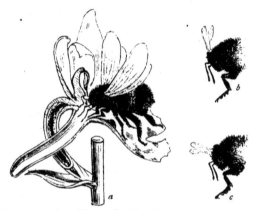

FIG. 57.— *a*, section of flower of orchis, shewing a bee standing upon the lip with its head touching the sticky gland to which the pollen masses are attached ; *b*, bee's head with the pollen masses erect, as removed ; *c*, the same with the pollen masses after they have moved forwards : all enlarged.

124. Birds with long slender bills, as humming-birds, and also great moths, thus fertilize long-tubed flowers; in all which and many other cases the adjustment of the parts of the flower to the form and habits of the insect or bird, and of these to the flower, is so accurate, that it is in vain to speculate whether the plant was adapted to feed the animal, or the animal adapted to fertilize the plant.

XXI.—THE FRUIT.

PERICARP, SEED.

125. The fruit consists of a covering (**seed-vessel**, or **pericarp**) containing one or more ripe seeds. The term should strictly apply to the result of the fertilization of one pistil, but it is extended to crowded masses of fruits belonging to several flowers on one peduncle or branch (mulberry Fig. 58, pine-cone). These are called aggregate fruits, or infructescences, just as the aggregates of flowers are called inflorescences (Par. 75). Further, various organs of the flower, or inflorescence, when retained on the fruit, are considered parts of the fruit; as the acorn-cup, which is formed of scale-like bracts (Par. 79); the flesh of the apple, hip, and pear, which are all formed of the swollen peduncle ; the strawberry (Fig. 64), which consists of a fleshy receptacle covered with ripe carpels ; and the fig (Fig. 59), which is a hollow fleshy peduncle containing many ripe carpels.

126. The study of the fruit is more complicated than that of any other organ of the plant, because : 1. of its composition, which can only be made out by an examination of the pistil (Sect. XVIII.); 2. because many parts visible in the pistil are often suppressed or masked in the fruit ; 3. because the seed is not always as distinguishable from the pericarp as the ovule always is from the ovary ; 4. because accessory organs are so often attached to it or envelope it ; 5. because carpels that are free in the pistil may become combined in the fruit ; 6. because the placentas (Par. 110)

sometimes grow out and form additional partitions in the cavity of the fruit.

127. The simplest classification of fruits is into :—
1. **pods**; these are dry, and their pericarp splits open along defined lines, or parts into separate pieces called **valves** (pea Fig. 61, wallflower Fig. 67); such are **dehiscent** fruits, their seeds fall out of the pericarp after it splits open. 2. Dry fruits that do not open by valves and are hence called **indehiscent**; the seeds of such do not fall out, but germinate within the pericarp, the embryo either throwing off the pericarp (maple), or its cotyledons remaining within it (acorn); of these there are two kinds, the **nut**, which is large and hard, and the **achene,** which is small and usually has a thin pericarp. 3. Indehiscent fleshy fruits, that either rot on the ground and thus set the seeds free, or are eaten by birds, which digest the flesh and reject the seeds (apple, holly, mistletoe, gooseberry). The chief kinds of these are the **berry,** which has a soft pericarp, and the **drupe,** of which the inner walls of the pericarp are hard and bony, or stony.

128. The above classification teaches nothing of the real nature of the fruit; the following does, and includes the chief kinds accessible to the student, who by learning all will obtain a better knowledge of fruits than he could by any other means. He should be careful to observe whether the fruit is inferior or superior (Par. 84 *d*), and further, in the cases of fruits that are composed of many combined dehiscent carpels, he should observe whether they split between the carpels (septicidal), or down their backs (loculicidal); or by the carpels parting from their axes (septifragal).

B. P.   G

In the following enumeration the character of the
seed is added to avoid subsequent repetition.

A.—Aggregate fruits or Infructescences (Par. 125).

Mulberry (Fig. 58).—A head of fruits, each consisting of a dry 1-seeded little indehiscent nut, inclosed
in four juicy perianth pieces.

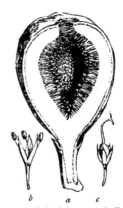

FIG. 58.—Aggregate fruit of
mulberry.

Fig. 59.—*a*, fruit of fig cut vertically;
b, male, and *c*, female flowers;
both much enlarged.

Fig (Fig. 59).—A hollowed-out fleshy peduncle,
with bracts at the top, containing innumerable fruits,
each consisting of a little 1-seeded indehiscent achene,
together with the withered remains of a perianth.

Pine-cone.—A series of woody scales, each with
two seeds at its base (here there is no pericarp, see
Par. 139).

B.—Simple fruits formed by the pistil of one flower.

(a) Indehiscent fruits of one carpel.

(1.) **Plum, Cherry.**—Fruit (a drupe) superior; pericarp of an outer very fleshy, and inner stony coat. Seed solitary, without albumen.

(2.) **Wheat.** (Fig. 12)—Fruit (an achene) superior; pericarp very thin, adhering so closely to the solitary seed that it cannot be separated. Seed albuminous. —In **oats** and **barley** the fruit is of the same structure, but inclosed in the hardened bracts (chaff).

(3.) **Nettle** (Fig. 60).—Fruit (an achene) minute, superior, flattened, dry, thin. Seed solitary, without albumen.

Fig. 60.—*a*, section of fruit of nettle much enlarged; *b*, section of seed of the same, showing the embryo, still more enlarged.

(4.) **Barberry.**—Fruit (a berry) superior; pericarp fleshy. Seeds 1 or 2, basal, albuminous.

Thistle (Fig. 42).—Fruit (an achene) crowned with a calyx formed of a tuft of silky hairs (pappus). Seed 1, basal, erect, without albumen.—In the **dandelion** (Fig. 41) the top of the fruit is drawn out into a long beak and crowned with a similar pappus. In the **daisy** the top of the fruit is obtuse and there is no pappus.

(b) Dehiscent fruits of one carpel (**pods**).

(5.) **Pea** (Fig. 61), **Bean.**—Fruit superior, dividing into 2 valves, with inner and outer line of dehiscence. Seeds many, without albumen, attached to

FIG. 61.—Fruit of pea splitting into two valves.

the line of dehiscence which is nearest to the free stamen (Fig. 47).

(6.) **Willow.**—Fruit superior, dividing into 2 valves. Seeds few, without albumen, basal, with long hairs at their bases.

(c) Indehiscent fruits of several free carpels.

Buttercup (Fig. 62).— Carpels many, dry (achenes), seated on a dry elevated receptacle. Seeds solitary in each achene, albuminous.

FIG. 62.—*a*, fruit of buttercup, cut open showing the seed ; *b*, seed of the same cut open showing the small embryo within the small albumen ; both much enlarged.

Bramble (Fig. 62), **Raspberry.**—Carpels many, fleshy (drupes), seated on a dry elevated receptacle. Seeds solitary, without albumen.

FIG. 63.-- Fruit of bramble with stamen and calyx beneath it.

Strawberry (Fig. 64).—Carpels many, dry (achenes), seated on a fleshy elevated receptacle. Seeds solitary, without albumen.

FIG. 64.—Fruit of strawberry with calyx and bracts beneath it.

Rose (Fig. 31).—Carpels few or many, dry (achenes), seated within the hollowed-out fleshy top of the peduncle. Seeds solitary, without albumen.

(*d*) *Indehiscent fruits of several combined carpels.*

Ash. — Fruit superior, dry, winged (a winged achene commonly called a key), of 2 combined carpels, 1-celled, each cell 1-seeded (one cell is sometimes suppressed). Seeds solitary, albuminous. —The **maple** fruit is of the same nature, but each carpel has a wing, and the two separate when ripe ; they do not, however, open so as to let the seed fall out.

Mallow (Fig. 65).—Fruit superior, a whorl of many 1-seeded carpels (achenes), combined by their faces. Seeds solitary, albuminous.

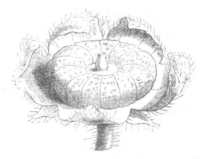

FIG. 65.—Fruit of mallow surrounded with the calyx, enlarged.

Deadnettle.—Fruit superior, of 4 dry achenes, each 1-seeded. Seeds albuminous.

Holly.—Fruit (a drupe) superior, fleshy, of 4 combined carpels, with four, 1-celled, 1-seeded stones. Seeds albuminous.

Olive.—Fruit (a drupe) superior, fleshy, of 2 carpels, forming a single 2-celled stone; cells 1-seeded. Seeds albuminous.

Potato.—Fruit (a berry) superior, of 2 fleshy carpels, 2-celled, with many seeds in each cell. Seeds albuminous.

Apple (Fig. 66).— Fruit 5-celled, of 5 carpels enveloped in the fleshy swollen top of the peduncle, each with a horny inner coat, and 1 or 2 seeds. Seeds without albumen.—(This, the quince, pear, &c., are called pomes.)

FIG. 66.—Fruit of apple cut across.

Gooseberry, Currant.—Fruit (a berry) inferior, of 2 fleshy carpels, 1-celled, with two placentas, and several seeds immersed in pulp.   Seeds albuminous.

Carrot, Parsnip.—Fruit inferior, of 2 combined dry carpels (achenes) that finally separate, each 1-seeded.   Seed albuminous.

Acorn.—Fruit (a nut) inferior, of 3 combined carpels, contained in a cup-shaped involucre (Par. 79); of these carpels one alone ripens, the others may be found as minute cavities at the top of the nut. Seed solitary, without albumen.— In the **beech,** the fruit is of the same structure, but three fruits are together included in a woody, 4-valved involucre, and each nut is 3-angled.—The sweet chestnut has the same structure as the beech. (The horse-chestnut is altogether different, see below.)—In the **hazlenut** also the fruit is of the same structure, but the pericarp is stony and the involucre green and leathery.

(e) Dehiscent fruits of several combined carpels.

Horse-Chestnut.—Fruit superior, of 3 carpels, combined into a globose, leathery, prickly, 3-celled pod, opening to the base by 3 valves. Seeds one in each cell, without albumen; cotyledons soldered together.

Primrose, Cowslip.—Fruit (a pod) superior, dry, of 5 carpels combined into a 1-celled pod, opening at the top by 5 valves. Seeds many, albuminous.

Violet (Fig. 53).—Fruit superior, dry, of 3 carpels, forming a 1-celled, 3-valved pod. Seeds many, albuminous.

Wallflower (Fig. 67).—Fruit superior, dry, of 2 carpels, forming a 2-celled pod, splitting to the base into 2 valves, which fall away from a framework. Seeds many, without albumen.

FIG. 67.—Pod of wallflower with one valve coming off.

Poppy.—Fruit superior, dry, of many carpels, forming a 1-celled pod, opening by small persistent valves under the stigma. Seeds many, albuminous.

Heath.—Fruit superior, dry, of 5 carpels, forming a 5-celled pod, the cells of which split longitudinally down the back. Seeds many, albuminous.

Rhododendron.—Similar to Heath, but the carpels separate from one another and from the central axis, and split longitudinally down the front (next the axis).

Iris, Crocus.—Fruit inferior, of 3 carpels, forming a 3-celled pod, the cells of which split longitudinally down the back. Seeds many, albuminous.

Orchis.—Fruit inferior, dry, of 3 carpels, forming a 1-celled pod, with 3 valves, which fall away from a framework. Seeds many, without albumen.

(f) Dehiscent fruits of several free carpels.

Columbine, Aconite, Larkspur.—Fruit superior, of 3 or more dry pods, splitting longitudinally down the inner face. Seeds numerous, albuminous.

129. The contrivances for the dispersion of fruits and for their becoming fixed to the ground, are very numerous, and afford most interesting studies. Many have winged appendages belonging to the carpels (maple, ash), or hooks by which they attach themselves to the fur of animals (cleavers), or wings formed of accessory organs (bracts of lime), or hooks, or spines (involucres of beech, chestnut, burdock). Others have fine hairs (pappus), formed by the calyx, (dandelion, thistle) ; others have a sticky surface, or one that gets sticky when the fruit falls on moist ground suitable for its germination (groundsel); whilst still others attract birds by their smell, colour, or sweetness, and are hence transported by them. Lastly, a few burst open with elastic force, the valves acting as pop-guns, and scattering the seeds abroad (balsam).

XXII.—THE SEED.

TESTA, ALBUMEN, EMBRYO.

130. The seed consists of the **embryo** (Par. 35)
and its coverings (**integuments**), and sometimes
albumen; it is the ovule fertilized and arrived at
maturity, at which period it has become independent
of the parent plant; it is attached to the pericarp by
a short or long cord, **funicle** (Par. 110), through
which it derived nourishment from the parent.

131. The **integuments** are usually double, the two
coverings sometimes corresponding to the two coats
of the ovule (Par. 114); the outer (**testa**) is generally
the harder and thicker, and is sometimes, but very
rarely, juicy (pomegranate). Two points should be
carefully noted on the testa — the scar (**hilum**)
indicating its point of attachment, and a minute
hole (**micropyle**) by which the pollen-tube entered
the ovule (Par. 114). The radicle of the embryo
almost always points to this hole. In some seeds
a ridge (**raphe**) passes from the funicle to the
opposite end of the seed, indicating the position of
the nourishing vessels that go to the base of the
nucleus (Par. 114), where they sometimes expand into
a dark spot. In many palm seeds the raphe sends
branches of vascular bundles through the testa.

132. The **embryo** is a rudimentary plant (Par. 35)
with partially-developed organs. The radicle of the
embryo is developed first, and is hence to be found
next the micropyle (Par. 131). When fully formed the

embryo consists of a cotyledon or cotyledons, a plumule, and a radicle; of these parts each cotyledon represents a leaf, the plumule and radicle together form an axis, of which the first is an ascending portion and becomes a stem, the latter a descending portion, giving origin to the root. The plumule is, in many plants, not developed till after germination.

There are two principal kinds of embryo amongst flowering plants, the mono- and di-cotyledonous; both have cotyledon, plumule, and radicle, but they differ most materially in their structure and mode of growth.

133. The monocotyledonous embryo is often a cylindrical body, of which the upper part is the cotyledon, and usually presents a longitudinal slit or depression in which the plumule lies, the lower part is the short, blunt radicle. In germination the plumule ascends, developing alternate, often sheathing, leaves; whilst the radicle either elongates for a short time and is then replaced by adventitious roots or is itself entirely undeveloped, but gives off sheathed adventitious roots (wheat, Fig. 12).

134. The dicotyledonous embryo is more complicated; its two cotyledons are often very large and equal and are always opposite, whilst the radicle is small and often short. The cotyledons may be thick (pea, horse-chestnut, acorn), or thin (maple), flat (castor-oil), or folded (mallow, mustard), or crumpled (convolvulus), veined with vascular bundles or not. The cotyledons may remain underground and suffer no change till they shrivel or decay (pea, bean, oak), or be carried up and become green leaves (mustard, Fig. 11) before the plumule is well developed. In germination the plumule

ascends, rarely developing sheathing leaves, and the radicle elongates and branches.

135. The **albumen** consists of a mass of cells containing starch, albuminoids (Pars. 17, 20), &c., provided for the nourishment of such embryos as possess it. It is usually formed within the embryo-sac (Par. 116). There is no organic connection whatever between the embryo and the albumen with which it is in contact, but yet the growing tissues of the former withdraw nourishing matter from the most distant part of the latter.

136. Seeds, like fruits (Par. 129), are provided with various means for aiding their dispersion, in the shape of accessory growths, colour, juicy coverings, &c. Many have the testa produced into a thin wing (pine-seeds), or are covered with long hairs (cotton), or have a tuft of hairs at one end (willow-herb), or at the base (willow); others become mucilaginous when moist, and thus adhere to the ground on alighting at a fit spot for growth (cress); or are supposed to attract birds by their brilliant colours, as certain tropical plants of the pea tribe, the pods of which open so as to expose the seeds; others have a juicy testa (pomegranate, magnolia, pæony); and still others, a fleshy cup or covering (an **aril**) formed by a growth from the funicle (Par. 130) (passion-flower and spindle-tree). The nutmeg-tree has a 1-seeded fruit like a peach, that splits open and exposes the nutmeg, surrounded by an aril of a brilliant scarlet colour: this aril no doubt attracts pigeons, which swallow the nutmegs, and transport them from island to island of the Moluccas.

137. The vitality of seeds is very variable as to

duration. Amongst instances of fugacious vitality are acorns, which germinate at once, and maple-seeds. As a proved instance of persistent vitality, the sacred bean of India is the most authentic ; one such taken from a herbarium upwards of one hundred years old, having germinated. Wheat is said to keep for seven years at the longest. The statements as to mummy wheat are wholly devoid of authenticity ; as are those of the raspberry seeds taken from a Roman tomb. On the other hand, that seeds may remain buried alive in the soil for many years is rendered most probable by the fact of charlock and broom appearing suddenly and in quantities in newly-turned-up soil that had not been disturbed for long periods. It is, however, difficult to believe that such a moist complex substance as living protoplasm can resist chemical change sufficiently long to favour the idea that seeds have lain buried alive in the soil for many hundred years.

XXIII.—SURFACE COVERINGS AND APPEN-DAGES.

138. These are either exudations from the cells of the epidermis (Par. 6), or modifications of the epidermal cells, or cellular growths from them. They serve very various and totally distinct functions, all necessary to the health, growth, or propagation of the plant. The principal of them may be most instructively classed under their apparent uses :—

(*a*) **Protective.**—The simplest of all is the bloom of the grape, cabbage-leaf, pea-pod, &c. It consists of a secretion of wax, which being insoluble in water probably intended to prevent its injurious effects on the subjacent tissues. Others are hairs and scales.

Hairs are either prolongations of epidermal cells, or single long cells of the epidermis (cotton), or strings of such cells (spider-wort). They are protections against wet, cold, and the effects of drought on the subjacent tissue. They are often branched (mallow) or radiate from a point, like a star; when the rays of such a star are combined the result is a scale or scurf (elæagnus.)

(*b*) **Defensive.**—The sting of the nettle is a single awl shaped rigid cell, with a swollen base, in which an irritating fluid is secreted. On piercing the skin the point breaks off, and the fluid is deposited in the wound.

(*c*) **Attractive.**—Hairs that secrete a fluid which is sugary or odorous are very common (sweet briar), and are no doubt intended to attract birds and insects for the purpose of fertilizing the flowers or carrying off and thus dispersing the seeds.

(*d*) **Nutritive.**—The glandular hairs of the sundew, which both retain the insects that visit the leaves (thus acting also as **detentive** organs) and absorb nutriment from them. The sticky stems of the catchfly, and many other plants, probably serve the same purpose.

(*e*) **Scansorial** (aids to climb).—Such are especially prickles, which are hooked cellular growths from the epidermis. By their aid the bramble and many roses climb bushes, and so get to the light. By their aid the rope-like rattan-canes of the Indies ascend the loftiest forest-trees, and expand their crown of foliage and flowers in the sun. They must not be confounded with spines (Par. 65).

XXIV.—GYMNOSPERMOUS PLANTS.

CONIFERS AND CYCADS.

139. There is a small but well-known group of flowering-plants that differs so much from all others that it requires to be described separately. Its principal members are the **coniferæ,** plants which include pines, firs, larches, cedars, yews, cypresses, junipers, araucarias, the wellingtonia, &c., and the **cycads,** palm-like plants of warm or hot countries. All are long-lived trees or shrubs, whose flowers have no perianth, and are almost invariably produced in male and female cones, consisting of scales, forming a close spiral round a woody axis. They are believed to have been inhabitants of the globe for a much longer period than any other flowering plants.

140. **Gymnosperms** resemble dicotyledons in the form and germination of the embryo, which however has often three or more cotyledons, in the exogenous growth of their stem (Par. 56), and they resemble all other flowering plants, in having stamens and ovules. They differ from dicotyledons in the layers of wood which are formed after the first year being destitute of vessels ; in the universal presence of disks with central pores on the wood-tissue ; and from all other flowering plants in the peculiar structure of the pollen, in the ovules not being inclosed in an ovary, and in the development of the embryo.

141. Their **stamens** for the most part consist of one or more anther-cells without filaments, situated on the under-surface of the scales of the male cone. Their **pollen** does not produce a tube from its inner

membrane (Sect. 108), but does so from a group of cells that form in its cavity.

142. Their **ovules** are borne on the upper surface of the scales of the female cone, which scales consist of an open carpellary leaf seated upon and combined with a bract (these are undistinguishable in the Scotch fir, but distinguishable in the larch). They resemble the ovules of flowering-plants, and like them may have one or two coats, and be straight or inverted through the unequal growth of one side (Par. 115). The embryo-sac becomes filled with cellular tissue at an early period. Within this tissue, beneath the uppermost layer of cells, forming the top of the sac, several larger cells appear and form as many **secondary embryo-sacs.** At the same time, that one cell of the uppermost layer which lies immediately above each secondary sac, divides longitudinally into four, leaving a canal between for the passage of the pollen tube.

143. **Fertilization** takes place by a pollen-grain, carried by the wind, alighting on the top of the nucleus of the exposed ovule, and sending its tube through the cellular substance of the nucleus, down to the primary embryo-sac. There it reaches the passage between the four cells above a secondary sac, traverses it, and touches the latter. On this contact taking place the contents of the secondary sac are divided by a transverse partition into two portions, the lower of which subsequently again divides and forms four filaments that descend into the tissue of the primary sac and nucleus. In the nucleus each filament begins to form an embryo by cell-division at its extremity, but only one embryo usually arrives at maturity.

144. Thus in gymnosperms, instead of the nucleus of the ovule containing a simple embryo-sac with one germinal vesicle which gives origin to an embryo, several secondary sacs are formed within the primary one, of which each gives origin to four embryos ; and as some gymnosperms have eight or more secondary embryo-sacs each producing four embryos, it follows that in such cases out of thirty-two commencements of embryos all but one are suppressed.

XXV.—CLASSIFICATION.

145. The objects of a **classification** of plants are, to place before the mind, in a clear manner, the relationships that· exist between them, and to express these relationships in precise terms, so that they may be communicated orally or in writing, and thus facilitate and advance a knowledge of plants.

146. The idea carried out in all methods of classifying plants is derived from the fact, that they appear to be related to one another as are the members of the human race, lineally and collaterally ; and whatever theory may be accepted for the origin of their kinds (**species**), the results obtained by classifying plants, and the mode of reasoning followed in detecting their relationships, are the same as what would follow were they proved to have descended from one or more common ancestors.

147. For the purposes of classification a **nomenclature** is essential, and that nomenclature is the best which conveys briefly and in expressive terms some distinguishing attribute of the plant or group of plants

to which its terms are applied. For this purpose
Latin and Greek are much used, because they are
acquired by educated people in all civilized countries,
and because they lend themselves by their flexibility
and. harmonious sounds to the compounding of
names.

148. The names in constant use for the purpose
of the classification of the members of the vegetable
kingdom are individual, variety, species, genus, order,
class, sub kingdom. When referring to a plant, its
generic and specific names are both used, putting
the generic first if the Latin language is used, and
the specific first if the English (as Rosa canina, Dog
rose).

A **species** is an aggregate of individuals which
have been proved to have descended from a common
ancestor, or are so similar to one another that they
may be presumed to have done so. But as no two
individuals are exactly alike, and as the number of
instances of unlikeness to the parent form increase
with the number of individuals produced by seed, it
becomes often difficult to define the limits of a species.
These unlike individuals are called **varieties** (Par.
150); and the descendants of a well-marked variety
that propagates its peculiarities with much constancy
by seed is called a **race,** and sometimes a **sub-
species.**

A **genus** is an assemblage of species resembling
one another in most important points of structure, as
the various kinds (species) of oak, elm, willow, &c.

Orders, also called **Families** are assemblages of
genera agreeing in certain marked characters. These
agreeing characters are sometimes obvious to the com-

mon observer, as those of the carrot and parsnip, which
are two genera of one order ; at other times they depend
on characters of flower and fruit that are not recognized
without botanical knowledge, as those of the buttercup and larkspur, which, though so unlike, are members
of one order.

Classes are groups of a still higher value, as those
of monocotyledon and dicotyledon. All classes are
grouped under the two **sub-kingdoms** of flowering
and flowerless plants which constitute the vegetable
kingdom.

149. **Individuality.** Plants, especially perennial
ones. are often regarded as composite beings, or aggregates of individuals, because their buds may be
detached and become separate individuals ; because
many parts annually die, and are replaced by similar
parts ; and because much of the substance of a tree
or bush dies and remains as dead matter throughout
the future life of the plant, forming a support as it
were for the fresh buds developed from the living
tissues that surround it. But whereas it is only of
some plants that the buds are capable of becoming
separate individuals, there are others of which single
cells are capable of playing the same part ; so that if
the answer to the question of " What is an individual
plant ? " is to depend on this power of its parts to
maintain a separate existence, it is a purely speculative
one, and we are reduced to accept the only alternative
of regarding each specimen as an individual, so long
as it remains an organic whole.

150. **Origin of Varieties.**—The result of cross-
fertilization (Par. 119) is that the qualities of two
distinct individuals are combined in the embryo and

H 2

appear in the future plant; whence it follows that the progeny of any individual plant which has been fertilized by another individual must differ more or less from that which bore it. Also seeds taken from different parts of the same plant being differently nourished will produce plants showing different amounts of unlikeness to the parent; and these sources of unlikeness are further affected by the conditions under which the seeds germinate and the future plant grows.

151. Profiting by these facts, gardeners highly manure certain plants, and cross-fertilize others, in order to obtain new strains, as they are called; and by raising plants from all the seeds that ripen under these conditions they obtain a large choice of individuals differing in various degrees from their parents.

152. Nature proceeds more slowly: very few indeed of the seeds shed in a state of nature produce plants that arrive at maturity; most perish from falling on stony ground; or from drought; or are eaten by beasts, birds, or insects; or if they grow, the young plants are choked or eaten, or otherwise killed. Of those that survive, such as have their parents' constitutions are the most numerous, and such will most resemble their parents in outward character. Hence marked variations, though so easily produced in a garden, are comparatively rare in a state of nature.

153. **Origin of Species.**—There are two opinions accepted as accounting for this; one, that of **independent creation,** that species were created under their present form, singly or in pairs or in numbers: the other, that of **evolution,** that all are the descendants of one or a few originally created simpler

third (No. 3) upside down over a tumbler of water with some of the leaves in the water, but the root exposed. In due time No. 1 will have faded; No. 2 will be quite fresh; No. 3 will have the parts not in the water faded. No. 1 shows that water contained in the plant has evaporated from its surfaces; No. 2 that the water has been absorbed by the root and conveyed to the leaves; No. 3 that the immersed leaves have not supplied the emerged portion of the plant with water.

157. **Decomposition of the carbonic acid of the air by plants in sunlight.**—Take a bunch of

Fig. 68

fresh green leaves—water-cresses answer well—and place them in a large bottle, then fill the bottle quite full of fresh spring water, so that no bubble of air is left in the bottle. Turn the mouth of the bottle, full of water and leaves, downwards into a basin full of water, and place the bottle and basin in the strong sunlight for an hour or two. If the leaves be then carefully examined they will be found to be covered with small bubbles, and that more of these bubbles

have collected at the top of the bottle. These
bubbles consist of pure oxygen gas derived from the
carbonic acid contained dissolved in the spring water.
This shows that plants have the power in presence
of sunlight of decomposing carbonic acid, taking
the carbon to build up their stems, leaves, &c., and
setting free the oxygen as a gas. Now repeat the
experiment ; but instead of placing the bottle of spring
water containing the leaves in the light, put it in a
dark cellar. There will then be no formation of
bubbles of oxygen gas, even after standing for many
hours. This shows that sunlight is necessary in order
that green plants may decompose carbonic acid, and
is therefore necessary for their growth.

158. **Respiration.**—In the green parts of plants
the giving off of carbonic acid gas, which takes place
in the respiration of all living things, is not observed
owing to the action of chlorophyll in decomposing
carbonic acid. It becomes, however, very evident in
parts which are not green.

Fill one-third of a wide-mouthed stoppered bottle of
rather less than two quarts capacity with soaked peas,
or with the expanding flower heads of camomile or
daisy. If the bottle is carefully opened after several
hours the air contained will be found to extinguish a
burning taper. This is due to the presence of carbonic
acid gas.

By taking special precautions and using a very
delicate thermometer, it is possible to show that a
distinct rise of temperature takes place during the
evolution of the carbonic acid. An illustration on a
large scale of this rise of temperature is afforded by
malt during its manufacture.

159. **Transpiration.**—Cut two branches of the same plant. Put one in a warm, the other in a cool place. Note that the former fades soonest. With a sufficiently delicate pair of scales this may be shown to arise from a larger loss of water. Evaporation proceeds more rapidly in warm air than in cold, because the former is able to hold a larger amount of moisture.

160. **Germination.**—Suspend an acorn or horse-chestnut by a piece of twine in the neck of a wide-mouthed bottle, and above the surface of some water. Place the bottle in a warm place. The water will evaporate and moisten the suspended seed, which will germinate. The condensed water is necessarily pure, and it is evident that this is the only material required by seeds in order to germinate.

Repeat the experiment with two sets of bottles; place some in a warm, others in a cooler place. Compare the time in which germination is effected.

161. **Effect of light on chlorophyll.**—Sow some cress seed, and keep the pots in a dark place. The seed-leaves will be pale. Remove part of the germinating plants to the light; the seed-leaves will become green. Compare their progress in this respect with those kept in the dark.

Press closely upon the surface of a geranium leaf some pieces of tin-foil, and afterwards expose the leaf for five to ten minutes to bright sunlight. The parts covered with the tin-foil will be found to have a darker colour than the rest. The lighter tint is due to the movement of the chlorophyll granules under the influence of light from the upper and lower surfaces of the cells to their sides.

162. **Colour of flowers independent of light.**

—Grow hyacinths of different colours in a completely dark cellar. They will expand their leaves and flowers. The former will be pale, but the latter will develop their proper colours.

163. **Heliotropism.**—Place a pot of germinating cress before a window. It will be found after a few days that the stems are turned in the direction of the light. This is due to the fact that light retards growth, and therefore the sides of the stem turned to the light and away from it come to have different lengths, and the stem consequently bends.

It follows from this that if a pot of germinating cress be shaded equally all round, the plants will grow faster than if not so shaded.

Grow some germinating cress in a closed box in one side of which a piece of dark blue glass has been introduced; there will be no curvature in the growth. Repeat the experiment substituting a piece of deep red glass; curvature will take place as with ordinary daylight. This proves that the heliotropic effect of light is due to the rays belonging to the red end of the spectrum.

XXVII.—A SCHOOL GARDEN OF FLOWERING PLANTS.

The following is a list of such easily procured and easily cultivated plants as will afford the teacher ample materials for instruction in Elementary Botany, will give an idea of the natural arrangements of flowering plants, and will convey a practical knowledge of many useful vegetables cultivated in all temperate regions.

This list is capable of indefinite extension according to the knowledge of the teacher, the size of the garden, the nature of its soils, the means at hand of procuring roots or seeds, and the labour that can be obtained for cultivating them. Abundant specimens of each should be grown, so that every pupil may have plenty to cut up and examine with the teacher.

The trees and shrubs marked with an asterisk (*) cannot well be introduced into such a garden amongst the herbaceous plants, but their names should be introduced in their proper places, and the pupil's attention should be directed to the plants themselves in neighbouring woods and plantations.

SERIES I.—**Angiosperms.** Flowering plants having the ovules inclosed in an ovary. Woody tissue containing abundant vessels.

CLASS I. DICOTYLEDONS.

DIVISION I.—Flowers usually with both a calyx and a corolla —the latter of free petals. Stamens inserted close under the ovary (not on the calyx). Ovary always superior.

Order *Ranunculaceæ.*—Clematis, anemone, butter-cup, hellebore, ficaria, columbine, larkspur, aconite, pæony.

Order *Berberideæ.*—Barberry.

Order *Papaveraceæ.*—Poppy, celandine.

Order *Fumariaceæ.*—Fumitory
Order *Cruciferæ.*—Stock, wallflower, arabis, cabbage, shepherd's
purse, honesty, mustard, cress, candy-tuft, sea-kale, radish,
charlock, turnip.
Order *Resedaceæ.*—Mignonette.
Order *Cistineæ.*—Rock-rose, gum cistus.
Order *Violareæ.*—Heartsease, dog-violet.
Order *Caryophylleæ.*—Pink, sweet william, catchfly, stitchwort,
spurrey, chickweed.
Order *Hypericineæ.*—Tutsan, St. John's-wort.
Order *Malvaceæ.*—Marsh mallow, lavatera, common mallow.
* Order *Tiliaceæ.*—Lime.
Order *Lineæ.*—Flax.
Order *Geraniaceæ.*—Crane's-bill, stork's-bill, pelargonium, tro-
pæolum, balsam.
Order *Vites.*—Grape-vine, Virginia-creeper.
* Order *Ilicineæ.*—Holly.

DIVISION II.—Characters of Division I., but stamens inserted
upon the calyx and ovary either inferior or superior.

* Order *Sapindaceæ.*—Maple, horse-chestnut.
* Order *Celestrineæ.*—Spindle-tree, buckthorn.
Order *Leguminosæ.*—Furze, broom, * laburnum, clover, lucerne,
saintfoin, pea, bean, vetch.
Order *Rosaceæ.*—* Plum, * cherry, spiræa, bramble, raspberry,
strawberry, cinquefoil, dog-rose, sweetbriar, * pear, * apple,
* hawthorn.
Order *Saxifrageæ.*—London pride, gooseberry, currant.
Order *Droseraceæ.*—Sundew.
Order *Crassulaceæ.*—Orpine, stone-crop, house leek.
Order *Onagrarieæ.*—Willow-herb, evening primrose, enchanter's
night-shade.
Order *Lythraceæ.*—Loose-strife.
Order *Cucurbitaceæ.*—Bryony, gourd.
Order *Umbelliferæ.*—Pennywort, hemlock, celery, caraway,
chervil, fennel, parsley, coriander, fools'-parsley, carrot,
parsnip, cow-parsnip.
Order *Araliaceæ.*—Ivy.
Order *Cornaceæ.*—Cornel, laurustinus.

DIVISION III.   COROLLIFLORAL.—Flowers with both calyx
and corolla, the latter usually of combined pieces. Stamens
usually inserted upon the corolla.

SUB-DIVISION I.—Ovary inferior.

Order *Caprifoliaceæ.*—Guelder-rose, elder, honeysuckle.

Order *Rubiaceæ.*—Madder, bedstraw, cleavers, woodruff.
Order *Valerianeæ.*—Valerian, corn-salad.
Order *Dipraceæ.*—Teazle, scabious.
Order *Compositæ.*—Cornflower, thistle, burdock, butter-bur, colts-
foot, single aster, daisy, golden rod, sun-flower, chamomile,
milfoil, corn marigold, tansy, wormwood, groundsel, chicory,
goatsbeard, lettuce, dandelion, sow-thistle, hawkweed.
Order *Campanulaceæ.*—Lobelia, rampion, campanula, Canter-
bury bell.
Order *Vacciniæ.*—Bilberry.

SUB-DIVISION 2.—Ovary superior.

Order *Ericaceæ.*—Arbutus, heath, ling, rhododendron.
Order *Oleineæ.*—Privet, *ash, lilac, jasmine.
Order *Apocyneæ.*—Periwinkle.
Order *Gentianeæ.*—Centaury, gentian.
Order *Polemoniaceæ.*—Jacob's ladder, phlox.
Order *Convolvulaceæ*—Convolvulus, dodder.
Order *Boragineæ.*—Bugloss, borage, comfrey, lungwort, forget-
me-not.
Order *Solaneæ.*—Henbane, nightshade, potato, deadly night-
shade, tobacco, thorn-apple.
Order *Plantagineæ.*—Plantain.
Order *Scrophularineæ.*—Mullein, toad-flax, snapdragon, mimulus,
foxglove, speedwell, yellow rattle.
Order *Labiatæ.*—Mint, marjoram, thyme, balm, sage, prunella,
horehound, deadnettle, rosemary.
Order *Verbenaceæ.*—Vervain.
Order *Primulaceæ.*—Primrose, cowslip, Lysimachia, pimpernel.
Order *Plumbagineæ.*—Thrift, statice.

DIVISION III.—Flowers with a single perianth.

Order *Polygoneæ.*—Bistort, buckwheat, dock, rhubarb.
Order *Chenopodiaceæ.*—Beet, spinach, goosefoot, orache.
Order *Thymeleæ.*—Daphne.
Order *Elæagneæ.*—Sea buckthorn.
Order *Aristolochieæ.*—Asarabacca, birthwort.
Order *Euphorbiaceæ.*—Spurge, castor oil, dog's mercury, box
Order *Urticeæ.*—Nettle, pellitory, *fig, *mulberry.
Order *Cannabineæ.*—Hop, hemp.
Order *Ulmaceæ.*—Elm.

DIVISION IV.—Flowers usually without obvious perianth.

Order *Salicineæ.*—Poplar, willow.
Order *Cupuliferæ.*—Oak, beech, hazel, hornbean, chestnut.

CLASS II.—MONOCOTYLEDONS.

DIVISION I.—Flowers with a distinct perianth.

SUB-DIVISION 1.—Perianth superior.

Order *Orchideæ.*—Orchis, helleborine, listera.
Order *Irideæ.*—Crocus, iris, gladiolus.
Order *Amaryllideæ.*—Narcissus, snowdrop.
Order *Dioscoreæ.*—Black bryony.

SUB-DIVISION 2.—Perianth inferior.

Order *Betulaceæ.*—Birch, alder.
Order *Alismaceæ.*—Water plantain, flowering rush.
Order *Liliaceæ.*—Asparagus, butcher's broom, lily of the valley,
    Solomon's seal, squill, star of Bethlehem, onion, fritillary,
    tiger lily, tulip, colchicum, crown imperial, hyacinth.
Order *Junceæ.* —Rush, wood-rush.

DIVISION II.—Flowers without a distinct perianth.

Order *Aroideæ.*—Cuckoo-pint.
Order *Typhaceæ.*—Bur reed, reed mace.
Order *Cyperaceæ.*—Bulrush, cotton-grass, galingale, sedge.
Order *Gramineæ.*—Foxtail-grass, canary grass, vernal grass,
    bent grass, millet grass, oat, reed, cocksfoot grass, couch
    grass, meadow grass, quaking grass, fescue grass, broom
    grass, wheat, barley, rye.

SERIES II.—**Gymnosperms.** Flowering plants with the
    ovules naked. Woody tissue destitute of vessels (except that
    of first year).

Order *Coniferæ.*—Juniper, * pine, yew, cypress, arbor-vitæ,
    * cedar, * larch, * spruce.

XXVIII.—SCHEDULES FOR EXERCISES ON LEAVES AND FLOWERS.

The first of these schedules is similar to that devised by the late Professor Henslow of Cambridge as a means of training the children of a village school in habits of accurate observation, by examining the structure of flowers. I have added one for leaves, which is even simpler and quite as useful for beginners; it is adapted for trees and shrubs, but may be extended and modified so as to embrace herbs, in which the stem- and root- leaves often differ in shape.

Blank schedules should be kept in great numbers and freely used by the pupils.

NAME OF PUPIL.	FLORAL SCHEDULE. BUTTER-CUP.		DATE AND PLACE WHERE GATHERED.	
Organ	No.	Insertion whether free or combined	Whether superior or inferior	Remarks
Calyx Sepals	5	free	inferior	green, hairy
Corolla Petals	5	free	inferior	yellow, shining
Stamens	many	free	inferior	crowded, with filaments
Pistil Carpels	many	free	superior on an elevated receptacle	crowded, in a round head, style o
Ovules or seeds in each carpel	1	at the base of the cavity		

NAME OF PUPIL	LEAF SCHEDULE				DATE.		
	lime	horse chestnut	soft grass	ash	oak	ivy	pear
Leaf of ...	lime	horse chestnut	soft grass	ash	oak	ivy	pear
Position and Stipulation	alternate exstipulate	opposite exstipulate	alternate exstipulate	alternate exstipulate	alternate stipulate	alternate exstipulate	alternate stipulate
Insertion	petioled	petioled	sessile on a sheath	petioled	petiole short or none	petioled	petioled
Division ...	simple	into seven leaflets	simple	pinnate	simple	simple	simple
Margins	serrate	serrate	entire	serrate	lobed	lobed	serrate
Surface ...	smooth	smooth	downy	smooth	smooth	smooth	downy
Veins ...	branching from a midrib	branching from a midrib	parallel through length of leaf	branching from a midrib	branching from a midrib	spreading from top of petiole	branching from a midrib

INDEX.

The plants enumerated below are, with few exceptions, easily procured, either from woods, fields, or shrubberies, or from gardens ; they should be used in a fresh state when possible, though many may be dried flat between paper so as to shew their instructive parts. Some, as wheat-ears, acorns, peas, &c., should be kept dry in quantities to be used for exercises ; others, as strawberries and such soft fruits, may be preserved in alcohol diluted with water. Lastly, a few objects must be had of a dealer who prepares slices of woods, starch grains, &c., for the microscope—these are marked with an asterisk (*).